Third World Debt: 362.51716

Towards an equitable solution

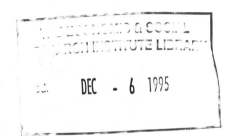

To

Mary, Cian and Philip

TMcC

Third World Debt:
Towards an equitable solution

Mary R. McCarthy and Thomas G. McCarthy

 TRÓCAIRE
and
GILL and MACMILLAN

Published in Ireland by

 TRÓCAIRE

Catholic Agency for World Development
169 Booterstown Ave.,
Blackrock, Co. Dublin
and Gill and Macmillan Ltd,
Goldenbridge, Inchicore, Dublin 8
with associated companies throughout the world.

© Trócaire 1994
ISBN 0 7171 1968 8

Index: Fergus Mulligan
Design: The Graphiconies
Print origination by Typeform Ltd.
Printed in Ireland by Genprint Ltd.

A catalogue record is available for this book from the British
Library.

Contents

		Page
List of Tables		6
Acknowledgements		7
PREFACE		9
Chapter 1:	Introduction	13
Part I:	**STATEMENT OF THE PROBLEM**	
Chapter 2:	The Magnitude of the Debt Problem	15
Chapter 3:	The Costs of Debt Crisis	27
Part II:	**RESPONSES**	
Chapter 4:	Plans and Initiatives	37
Chapter 5:	A Sample of Opinion	65
Part III:	**TOWARDS AN EQUITABLE SOLUTION**	
Chapter 6:	The Idea of Fairness	79
Chapter 7:	Fairness in Current Proposals	95
Chapter 8:	Recommendations	113
Appendix I:	Main Sources of International Statistics on External Third World Debt	117
Appendix II:	Sources of Financial Flows to Developing Countries	121
Glossary of Abbreviations		130
Bibliography		134
Index		141

List of Tables

2.1 Debt Indicators for Developing Countries, 1983-91
(in %) 16

2.2 Main Economic Indicators, 1983-91: Developing
Countries and Industrial Countries, (average annual
changes (%) and $bn) 18

2.3 Debt Indicators for Two Developing Country Groups
(in %) 19

2.4 Main Economic Indicators, 1983-91: Developing
Country Groups, (average annual changes (%) and $bn) 21

2.5 External Debt by Maturity and Class of Creditor,
1983-91: All Developing Countries and Country
Groups, (% of total and $bn) 23

3.1 Gross Capital Formation (GCF) as % of GDP,
Annual Rate of Change (%) of GDP and GDP
per capita, Central Government Fiscal Balances
(CGFB) as % of GDP and Annual Rate of Change
(%) in Consumer Prices (INF): 15 HICs and
Sub-Saharan Africa, 1988-89 31

Acknowledgments

We would like to express our warmest appreciation to Mary Sutton of Trócaire for assistance with this project. Both authors had little experience with developing country issues prior to undertaking this study. We quickly came to value Mary's knowledge and insight. She was generous with her time and diplomatic with her overtures for finished copy.

Alan Matthews of Trinity College Dublin and Frank Barry of University College Dublin gave written and verbal comments that helped focus the study. They, along with Mary Sutton, provided very helpful encouragement. We are also grateful to the other members of the Trócaire Research Advisory Group who gave written comments.

Mrs Mary Riordan of the Development Library at University College Dublin gave us valuable assistance with literature searches and particularly with gathering information from official agencies.

Tom McCarthy would like to thank seminar participants at The Queen's University, Belfast (Development Studies Association, September 1989) and at the Columban Missionaries in Co. Meath. A long discussion with Peadar Kirby was also most useful in tying up some loose ends.

The task of guiding the project to publication fell to Andy Storey and we thank him for this and his help in updating data and references.

M.R.McC
T.G.McC

Preface

This book makes a very valuable contribution to our understanding of the so-called Third World debt crisis. In 1990 the developing world owed $1,340 billion to its foreign creditors. This represented around half the total income of the developing world, or $327 for every person in that world. Despite enormous and painful debt repayments during the 1980s, the developing world's debt burden in 1990 was significantly higher than in 1982, the year when the debt crisis "started".

The Third World debt crisis exploded into the public gaze on 30 August 1982, when Mexico suspended repayments on its foreign debt (owed to 1,400 different foreign banks). By the end of 1982 a total of 35 developing countries were overdue in their debt repayments, prompting a flurry of "rescheduling" negotiations (involving changes in the timing and conditions of repayment).

The causes of the crisis lay in the 1970s. After oil prices rose five-fold in 1973, the oil-rich countries of OPEC invested their new found wealth in the western banking system, which in turn lent the money out to money-hungry poor countries. Flush with this new money the western bankers were far from cautious in their lending strategies – many projects were financed which were of dubious value and which were unlikely to generate the income necessary to sustain repayments.

At that time it seemed like a fairly sensible strategy from the point of view of the borrowers – in particular, interest rates were low so the repayment burden appeared likely to be bearable (even if some of the projects financed were of questionable usefulness). But in the early 1980s interest rates unexpectedly rocketed upwards, mainly in response to the spendthrift economic policies of the Reagan presidency in the USA.

Two other factors contributed to the emergence of a crisis: the value of the dollar rose, which added to the burden because much of the debt had to be repaid in dollars; and the prices for the exports (such as copper and cocoa), which developing countries depended on for their foreign exchange, slumped. For example, the world price of cotton fell by 32 per cent between 1980 and 1988. Latin America's terms of trade – the average price of exports compared to the average price of imports – declined by 30 per cent in the 1980s; in Africa the fall was 40 per cent.

So the debtor countries found themselves in a crisis, largely because of factors outside their control. At the end of the 1980s the foreign debt of many Latin American and African countries was equal to 300 per cent of their export earnings. This was despite the fact that enormous repayments were made: the problem was that many countries were simply borrowing to repay their debts. For this reason, Latin America's debt increased from $243 billion in 1980 to $434 billion in 1989, despite repayments of $472 billion over that period.

However, throughout the 1980s, efforts to repay at least some of the debt in real terms (rather than simply through new borrowing) imposed severe costs on many countries as government expenditure was slashed and the stress was placed on production for export. Such policies were a major factor in explaining how Latin America came to send $200 billion more to the developed countries during the 1980s than it received from those countries through aid, new loans and other sources.

As a result of these policies, health and education expenditure fell in much of the developing world during the 1980s. Real wages declined, and living standards were further eroded by measures such as the abolition of food subsidies. The results included higher infant and child mortality rates and increased malnutrition. Factors other than debt also played a role here, especially the general effects of the worldwide recession, but the debt crisis was directly responsible for much of the human devastation which ravaged the developing world in the 1980s.

Despite the panic in Western financial circles over the possibility of non-repayment, the Western banks did quite well during this period – they continued to receive a steady flow of repayments and there were no major defaults. It has now been recognised that cancelling at least some of the debt will not bring the entire capitalist system crashing down. Official schemes currently in operation accept the principle of limited debt relief (i.e., not having to pay back the whole sum).

All indebted countries do not face identical problems. The "middle-income" debtors (mainly in Latin America), who owe most of their debt to commercial banks, have seen their situation improve somewhat in recent years. They have benefited to some extent from the debt reduction deals negotiated under the so-called Brady Plan, reflecting the importance attached by the West to restoring growth and expanding markets in these countries. Bush's Enterprise for the Americas initiative, proposing moves towards free trade throughout North and South America, and also involving debt relief, similarly reflects the desire to expand opportunities for US business. Quite simply, economies crippled by debt are poor business partners.

By contrast, the situation of the low-income debtors (mostly in Africa), who owe most of their debt to western governments and official institutions, is worsening: on average, the debt of these poor African countries represents 500 per cent of their export earnings. In practice, many such countries repay less than half the sums due and thus accumulate enormous arrears. The lack of progress in resolving the problems of these countries reflects the low economic importance the West accords Africa – unlike Latin America, market and investment opportunities in Africa are seen, for the most part, as worthy of little attention.

The mechanisms which developing countries were forced to adopt to deal with the debt crisis fell under the general heading of structural adjustment. Implemented under the supervision of the World Bank and/or the International Monetary Fund (IMF), structural adjustment in the 1980s was characterised by the following components:

- reduced public expenditure;
- a reduced role for the state in the economy e.g., through privatisation;
- liberalisation of the economy e.g., removing price controls;
- exchange rate devaluation;
- export promotion;
- openness to foreign investment.

The harmful effects of some of these policies, in terms, for example, of health and education spending cut-backs, have been mentioned above. Developing country governments were forced to adopt these policies in order to retain access to sources of international lending, and more recently in order to qualify for whatever debt relief was on offer.

All of these issues are excellently outlined in this book.

At one level the reason why western governments promoted structural adjustment is clear enough: policies such as export promotion and public expenditure reductions ensured that developing countries were able to service their debts and thus uphold the profits of western lenders.

But, it can be argued, there may be a deeper ideological justification for the continued insistence on the adoption of structural adjustment in the Third World, which is related to the accelerating globalisation of free markets and free trade. This free market/trade mode was promoted through the medium of the GATT negotiations, and also though the conditions imposed on loans and aid by the IMF, other multilateral bodies and governments. The conditions countries now have to fulfil in order to qualify for debt relief are another example of the way in which the model can be "pushed".

Although there are serious doubts about the ability of this model to regenerate Third World economies, free markets certainly suit the interests of Western capital in terms of increasing market and investment opportunities (which, as noted above, are more plentiful in Latin America than in Africa). This is not to argue for the existence of a conscious conspiracy on the part of Western actors, but it is hardly surprising that many Third World commentators have come to see the debt crisis as a mechanism for recolonisation.

It is ironic that, from being the source of a potential crash for the capitalist world at the beginning of the 1980s, the debt crisis has been transformed into a mechanism for imposing policies on the developing world which are favourable to the interests of western businesses.

A more equitable solution is long overdue – this book points to how such a solution might be achieved.

Justin Kilcullen
Director, Trócaire
May 1994

Chapter 1

Introduction

This study concerns what is commonly referred to as the Third World Debt problem. This is somewhat of a misnomer, however, since the debt burden poses problems well beyond the borders of these countries. As a consequence the search for a solution to the problem concerns the industrial as well as the debt distressed countries themselves.

If one single reason can be identified as the motivation for the study, it would be the fact of net transfers from developing to developed countries that has emerged in recent years. This has given rise to widespread alarm. The view that past attempts at solving the debt problem have been more concerned with limiting the exposure of creditor banks while ignoring the interests of debtors has gathered momentum. This statistic has induced interest groups such as the Catholic Church and non-governmental organisations (NGOs) to call for an "ethical" solution to the debt problem. A central aspect of such a solution would be that debtors be treated in an equitable fashion.

The objective of this study is to identify the nature of an equitable solution to the debt problem. We use the term equity rather than ethics. Our conception of equity, however, is grounded on principles of ethics. The set of ethical principles we adopt is narrow. Some may, as a consequence, argue that we employ too narrow a conception of ethics. We defend our approach on two grounds. In the first place, we believe that the set of ethical principles from which we work is more likely to meet with universal approval. Secondly, our training as economists leads us to believe that such an approach is more conducive to coherent analysis.

The study is divided into three parts. In Part I we outline the nature of the debt problem. This is done at two levels. In Chapter 2 we use statistics to illustrate the state of indebtedness. Then in Chapter 3 we attempt to measure the cost of debt by focusing on its effect on the populations of these countries.

In Part II we look at the responses to the debt problem. Chapter 4 reviews the plans and initiatives that have emerged.

Our objective here is to present these proposed solutions in a typological framework while at the same time drawing out the context in which they emerged. This is followed in Chapter 5 by a discussion of the opinions held by various parties to the debt problem. The discussion is by necessity rather cursory since an analysis of evolving opinion would merit a separate study of its own.

Our analysis of equity in alleviating the debt problem is contained in Part III. We begin in Chapter 6 by formalising the concept of equity we adopt. This leads to the identification of a set of criteria which are applied in Chapter 7. This Chapter contains an analysis of the case for debt reduction along with an examination of the approach and mechanics of an equitable solution. In this way we identify a set of recommendations for the implementation of such a solution. These recommendations are summarised in Chapter 8.

One of the main difficulties in undertaking a study of the debt problem is in deciding where to set limits. It would not be inappropriate to consider the whole question of development and the approach to this in the developed world. For practical purposes this was not possible.

Another difficulty we confronted was the fact that changes in the approach adopted by the industrial countries to the debt problem occurred during the course of the study. We have attempted to take account of as much of this as possible. Much of our comment will no doubt become dated. However, by concentrating on principles in Part III we hope that this monograph will provide a more enduring guide to those considering an equitable resolution of the debt problem.

Chapter 2

The Magnitude of the Debt Problem

Introduction

The inauguration of what has become known as the international debt crisis is marked by Mexico's announcement on 30 August 1982 of a temporary suspension of payments of approximately $13 billion (owed to about 1400 foreign banks) on an external debt of $84 billion. By the end of 1982, the debt payments of around 35 developing countries were overdue and a record number of negotiations to reschedule the payments were in progress. As with many crisis events, a post-event analysis of the period leading up to the crisis dispels the notion of the suddenness of the events as characterised by the media. Rather than reanalyse here the origins of the debt crisis, which have been discussed at great length elsewhere (see, for example, Cline 1984) we have chosen to begin by describing the current state of affairs and the relative performance of some developing country regions over time. Our emphasis is on the 1980s, as the figures for that decade are the most conclusive available. We follow this with a brief analysis of the composition of debt in the Third World.

The Current State of Affairs

According to the IMF *World Economic Outlook* of May 1992, at the end of 1991 the total external debt of developing countries[1] reached $1,513 billion or 32.1% of aggregate GDP. While this represents an increase on the corresponding figure in 1982, when the debt to GDP ratio was 31.0%, it is also an improvement on the ratio of almost 39% of GDP recorded for 1986 and 1987. The other broad debt indicators have also shown some signs of improvement since 1987.

Table 2.1: Debt indicators for developing countries, 1983-1991 (in %)

Indicator	1983	1984	1985	1986	1987	1988	1989	1990	1991
Ratio of:									
Debt to GDP	32.9	33.9	36.4	39.0	38.5	36.4	33.3	31.5	32.1
Debt to Exports	135.0	137.0	154.5	180.4	167.0	148.2	135.3	126.0	125.7
Debt Service[a] to Exports	18.2	19.3	20.9	22.5	20.1	18.8	16.3	14.3	14.2
Interest Service to Exports	10.8	11.5	12.0	12.4	9.2	9.3	8.2	7.0	7.1

Source: IMF *World Economic Outlook*, May 1992
Notes: a Debt service payments = principal repayments plus interest payments.

The ratio of debt to GDP and the ratios of debt, debt service and interest service payments to exports have all fallen slightly since 1986. The latter ratio is considered to be a good indicator of a country's ability to finance its debt because principal repayments and interest payments on the external debt have to be made in foreign currencies and earnings from exports provide one source of such foreign exchange. While it may be possible to reschedule the repayments of the principal, interest payments must be made if the country is to maintain its creditworthiness. So the interest payments-to-exports ratio provides an indication of the proportion of export earnings which must be used to meet the country's on-going obligation in relation to its external debt. Consequently, the decline in the ratio might be viewed favourably in the struggle to contain the debt problem.

However, any such optimism should be tempered by a more detailed analysis of the situation. Firstly, the ratio gives a misleading impression for the following reason. Nominal interest rates, which had been on a downward trend from 1982 to 1987, increased in 1988-89. The real cost of debt is assessed in terms of the real interest rate and the real interest rate for developing countries is the nominal LIBOR rate (London Inter Bank Offered Rate) less the rate of change in the export price index for developing countries. High nominal interest rates and declining export prices kept real interest rates high between 1982 and 1985. Falling nominal interest rates and rising export prices lowered the real cost of external debt to developing countries in 1986 and 1987 but this trend has been reversed thereafter.

Secondly, the unilateral withholding of debt service payments by debtor countries, such as Brazil, must take some credit (however small) in explaining the fall in the interest payments to exports ratio. This point raises another issue which should be borne in mind in interpreting all of the tables which contain figures relating to principal repayments and interest payments on external debt. It is that the figures for debt service and interest service payments are based on ex post payments. As such, these figures generally underestimate the scheduled payments for these years. For example, the a priori figures for debt service to exports and interest payments to exports in 1987 were 23.2% (as opposed to the actual value of 20.1%) and 10.4% (as compared to 9.2%) respectively.

The relative economic performance of developing countries

An assessment of the real cost of external debt cannot rely on a single indicator. There are other indications that the costs of adjustment, in terms of the impact on present and future living standards of domestic policies aimed at containing (if not reducing) the debt burden, have been high in developing countries. An insight into the macroeconomic performance of developing countries as compared with industrialised countries is provided by Table 2.2

The growth rate of real GDP[2] continues to be volatile in both developing and industrialised countries, with the estimates for 1991 indicating a sharp downturn for the developing countries especially. The divergence in consumer price index (CPI) inflation rates between the two groups is much more striking – the rate increased from 36.4% in 1987 in developing countries to 80% in 1990 while the corresponding figures for the industrialised countries are 3.0% and 4.9%, respectively. Despite the growth of real GDP (which may give a misleading impression of a country's economic well-being, as we shall see later), the rapid (if temporary) acceleration in the inflation rate and the stagnation in the current account of the balance of payments do not bode well for the developing countries' economies. Such figures are even more striking at the level of individual debtor countries or country groupings to which we now turn our attention.

Table 2.2: Main economic indicators, 1983-91: developing countries and industrial countries
(average annual changes (%) and $bn)

Indicator	1983	1984	1985	1986	1987	1988	1989	1990	1991
Rate of growth of real GDP (%)									
Developing	2.2	4.2	3.7	3.7	3.9	4.1	3.2	1.3	-3.4
Industrial	2.7	4.5	3.3	2.8	3.2	4.3	3.4	2.5	0.8
CPI inflation Rate (%)									
Developing	32.7	37.8	34.3	27.9	36.4	57.2	71.1	80.0	41.4
Industrial	5.0	4.7	4.2	2.4	3.0	3.3	4.4	4.9	4.4
BOP on current account ($bn)a									
Developing	-57.8	-31.7	-24.9	-46.4	-3.9	-22.4	-18.4	-7.9	-84.8
Industrial	-24.5	-53.8	-62.5	-27.7	-54.8	-53.9	-81.5	-97.5	-27.9

Source: IMF *World Economic Outlook*, May 1992
Note: a = includes official transfers

Much attention has been devoted to two IMF/World Bank country groupings: the 15 middle-income countries designated as heavily indebted countries (HICs) by virtue of their high debt and debt service ratios and the 43 countries comprising the geographical unit of Sub-Saharan Africa (SSA).[3] Although we have followed the tradition of focusing on these two groups, we note that they do not include all of the developing debtor countries which have severe debt burdens. There are several other low- and middle-income "borderline-highly-indebted" countries[4] which account for about 20% of the total outstanding external debt and which should also be considered in any plans to alleviate the debt crisis.

The nature of the debt problem differs between the HICs and SSA for a number of reasons. First, World Bank estimates put the HICs share of total developing country medium- and long-term external debt at close on 54% and the SSA share at approximately 12% in 1988. Secondly, almost all of SSA's external debt is public or publically-guaranteed with a much higher proportion owed to official creditors[5] and less to commercial banks and other private creditors than is the case in the HICs (see Table 2.5 for further details). Furthermore, a larger share of SSA's debt is on concessional terms (for example, loans with below market interest rates and long repayment periods) and the grant element is almost five times larger than for the HICs. Thirdly, although the SSA share of total developing country external debt is smaller, the burden facing countries in SSA is large when compared with their respective economic capacities.[6] For example, the majority of countries in the HIC group is classified by the World Bank as middle-income, i.e. countries in which the GNP per capita in 1985 was $401 or more, while most of the SSA countries are categorised as low-income, i.e. countries where GNP per head was less than or equal to $400 in 1985. In addition, the SSA countries lack a diversified export base when compared with the HICs.

Table 2.3 presents the summary debt indicators for these two groups.

The ratio of debt to GDP has fallen in the HICs. One of the main reasons for the slowdown in debt accumulation since 1988 is the increased use of instruments to reduce debt. Debt reduction instruments (which will be discussed in more detail in Chapter 4) allow creditors to transfer ownership of debt, change the nature of their claims, or alter the financial profile of their assets. The World Bank estimates that such transactions reduced the face value of the debt by $8 billion in 1987 and $22 billion in 1988 alone. The major development affecting these countries has been the negotiation of agreements on debt reduction under the Brady Plan. It is as yet too soon to assess fully the effects of these agreements.

Table 2.3: Debt indicators for two developing country groups (in %)

Indicator	15 Highly Indebted Countries			Sub-Saharan Africa[a]		
	1980-86	1987	1991	1980-86	1987	1991
Ratio of:						
Debt to GDP	42.3	58.8	41.2	52.2	92.6	83.6
Debt to Exports	267.0	365.3	378.7	229.6	332.9	253.0
Debt Service to Exports	40.0	37.4	30.6	22.1	21.6	22.0
Interest Service to Exports	26.3	20.7	17.1	10.2	9.1	10.7

Source: IMF *World Economic Outlook*, May 1992
Note: a = excluding Nigeria

The larger Latin American countries have, for one reason or another, appeared as the centre of attention in the group. Brazil, Latin America's largest debtor, progressed from declaring a moratorium on interest payments to the commercial banks to being completely current on all interest payments, to an $82 billion debt rescheduling package, signed in November 1988. No interest was paid on the $120 billion external debt after July 1989. Mexico, on the other hand, whose adjustment policies (particularly in terms of promoting free movements of goods and services in and out of the country[7]) have been cited as a "good example" for other Latin American countries, negotiated an emergency loan package of $3.5 billion from the US government in October, 1988. Mexico was also the first developing country to negotiate an agreement on debt reduction with its commercial bank creditors under the Brady Plan. This agreement reduced its outstanding liabilities by $6.8 billion and its debt service payments by an additional $22.5 billion, resulting in a yearly saving of $1.46 billion.

The broad directions of change in the debt indicators in SSA are the same as those in the HICs, although the levels of these indicators are vastly different. Debt service ratios are lower mainly because of lower interest rates and easier access to debt rescheduling facilities. Despite the special economic reform programmes introduced in most of the SSA countries, the prospects for debt-containment remain dismal. The 1978 United Nations Conference on Trade and Development (UNCTAD) resolution to convert official debt into grants led to a 3% reduction in total outstanding debt by the end of 1988. However, the debt, debt service and interest service ratios to exports have continued to increase, or at least hardly fall. These rises, despite debt cancellations, reschedulings and debt relief on concessional terms by Paris Club[8] creditors in line with the terms of the 1988 Toronto Summit, may be attributed to: the fact that most debt cancellations pertained to concessional debt with little interest service requirements with little or no change in commercial bank debt which carries a large share of the debt service; continued official concessional lending and poor growth in the value of exports.

Contrary to the HIC group, individual countries are rarely highlighted as special cases in SSA. However, while the SSA countries all share similar problems of structural weakness (such as a narrow export base, rapid population growth, poor health and education services, etc), some countries are more debt-distressed than others. In 1988, the debt to GNP ratios of 50%

(17) of these countries exceeded 100%. Notable among these were the ratios of 281% for Guinea-Bissau, 294% for Mozambique and 289% for Zambia. For Madagascar and Niger, the long-term debt service to exports ratios were 35% and 34% in 1988. Besides the extension of World Bank and IMF programmes to aid adjustment and promote debt relief, the main initiative for debt relief in low-income African countries has been the June 1988 Toronto Summit. This allowed the non-concessional bilateral official debt of low-income African countries, following IMF/World Bank supported adjustment policies, to reschedule this debt under a menu with concessional options. As in the case of the Brady Plan, it is too soon to fully assess the long-term effects of such agreements.

Table 2.4: Main economic indicators, 1983-91: developing country groups (average annual changes (%) and $bn)

Indicator	1983	1984	1985	1986	1987	1988	1989	1990	1991
Rate of growth of real GDP (%):									
15 HICs	-2.9	2.3	3.8	4.2	1.7	1.5	1.3	-0.5	0.6
Sub-Saharan Africa[a]	-0.2	2.3	3.6	3.4	2.0	2.8	1.7	1.1	1.4
Rate of growth of real per capita GDP (%):									
15 HICs	-4.9	0.3	1.7	1.0	0.5	-0.6	-1.0	-2.4	-1.4
Sub-Saharan Africa[a]	-3.1	-0.7	0.6	0.4	-1.0	-0.2	-1.3	-1.9	-1.8
CPI inflation rate (%)									
15 HICs	90.9	112.2	108.1	68.5	104.4	217.4	425.4	574.5	158.0
Sub-Saharan Africa[a]	25.6	24.2	18.5	18.9	22.0	20.6	21.9	21.0	35.1
BOP on current account ($bn)									
15 HICs	-15.3	-0.9	-0.4	-17.4	-7.8	-8.4	-4.3	-2.0	-23.8
Sub-Saharan Africa[a]	-5.6	-3.2	-3.4	-5.6	-6.4	-7.5	-6.3	-7.7	-7.7

Source: IMF *World Economic Outlook*, May 1992
Note: a = excluding Nigeria

Other economic indicators in the two country groupings do little to produce a more favourable picture. From Table 2.4, it is clear that while the rate of growth of real GDP was mostly positive in both the HICs and SSA, real GDP per capita has fallen. This highlights the problem in relying on the growth of real GDP alone as an indicator of economic well-being. Inflation, which had slowed down somewhat in the HICs, accelerated sharply to 574.5% in 1990. This reappearance of chronic inflation rates in some countries, such as Argentina, Brazil and Peru led to some disquiet and hampered any negotiation to reduce their debt burdens. Although the balance of trade (BOT) in the HICs is in surplus, the current account of the balance of payments (BOP) remains in deficit in both groups. This is attributable in part to the continued decline in the prices of primary commodities, such as coffee and cocoa, on which many African countries depend for export earnings. On the other hand, the prices of imports from the industrialised world have continued to rise and, in spite of the efforts made by many countries to cut imports, this has compounded the problem of achieving a current account surplus on the balance of payments. Net transfers (i.e. repayments of existing loans plus interest payments less new loans) from Africa to the IMF of $1 billion in 1987 further exacerbated the situation. It comes as no surprise then that real per capita income in these countries has continued to fall. These aggregate figures conceal even more bleak outlooks at the individual country level. For example, in 1988, Sudan, with a GNP per capita of $340, had a total debt of $11.8 billion, a debt to exports ratio in excess of 900% and a scheduled debt service payments to exports ratio for 1989 of 68%.

Composition of external debt in the Third World

One of the distinguishing features of the debt problem in SSA as compared to the HICs has been that the major part of the debt claims of the former has been concentrated in the hands of official creditors (i.e. international organisations[9] and governments and government agencies), while most of the debt was owed to commercial creditors (mainly banks) in the latter.

From Table 2.5, it is clear that: official creditors have consolidated their position as the main creditor for debt in Sub-Saharan Africa over the past few years; while financial institutions[10] have decreased their shares of debt in both country groups, they continue to be the main creditor in the 15 HICs; and the distribution of long-term debt among official creditors, financial institutions, and other private creditors[11] is much more diversified for the 15 HICs than for the Sub-Saharan African group.

Table 2.5: External debt by maturity and class of creditor, 1983-91: All developing countries and country groups.
(% of total and $ billion)

Indicator	1983	1984	1985	1986	1987	1988	1989	1990	1991
ALL DEVELOPING COUNTRIES:									
External debt									
$bn	887	879	949	1050	1173	1194	1221	1281	1348
Long-term debt(%)	80.5	80.6	82.0	83.3	83.2	82.9	82.3	81.7	82.1
% of Total									
Long-term debt to:									
Official creditors	31.7	31.7	34.1	36.3	39.1	39.8	41.2	42.8	42.3
Financial institutions	51.6	50.4	48.0	45.7	44.2	42.3	40.6	38.8	38.9
Other private creditors	16.7	17.9	17.9	18.0	16.7	17.9	18.2	18.4	18.8
15 HEAVILY INDEBTED COUNTRIES:									
Long-term debt									
$bn	339	360	377	403	441	430	425	429	435
% of total debt	85.6	88.4	90.0	91.2	90.9	90.7	89.4	87.5	88.0
% total debt to:									
Official creditors	16.2	17.9	21.5	24.1	27.3	29.1	31.9	36.8	36.9
Financial institutions	68.5	69.7	67.0	65.4	62.9	60.1	58.3	53.7	53.8
Other private creditors	15.3	12.4	11.5	10.5	9.8	10.8	9.8	9.5	9.2
SUB-SAHARAN AFRICA:[a]									
Long-term debt									
$bn	50.1	50.2	57.8	77.7	92.9	97.3	100.2	112.3	117.5
% of total debt	89.1	89.3	89.3	89.8	88.3	88.2	88.0	89.1	89.4
% of total debt to:									
Official creditors	63.0	66.5	68.6	69.2	69.0	70.4	69.4	71.4	73.4
Financial institutions	24.9	22.8	21.2	18.4	18.1	16.7	16.1	16.7	16.7
Other private creditors	12.1	10.7	10.0	12.4	12.9	13.1	14.5	11.8	10.0

Source: IMF World Economic Outlook, May 1992
Note: a = excluding Nigeria

Official debt is broadly categorised as multilateral and bilateral. About 60% of official claims in SSA in 1988 were bilateral claims, of which 77% was held by OECD countries and the remainder by

OPEC, Council for Mutual Economic Assistance (CMEA) and other countries. The multilateral debt is accounted for principally by the World Bank and the IMF, whose share of total official debt grew throughout the 1980s. The burden of servicing multilateral debt (and IMF debt in particular) has also grown.

Although commercial bank claims represent only a small part of total external debt, they should not be ignored for a number of reasons. First, in a few countries, these claims are responsible for a large share of the debt service paid and interest rescheduling is often resisted by the banks. Secondly, any rescheduling which does take place may be accompanied by higher interest rates.

In 1980 non-concessional loans, i.e. loans where the rate of interest and other terms are market-determined, provided over half (57.7%) of total external financing to developing countries. By 1986, this share had dropped to 35% and Official Development Assistance (ODA) had increased from 28% to 42%. ODA is defined by the Development Assistance Committee (DAC) of the OECD (see Appendix II) as financial flows to developing countries which carry a grant element of at least 25%. Direct private investment (DPI), defined as the purchase of ownership and control of a company in a country by a foreign private individual or entity, doubled between 1980 and 1986 and net capital flows changed from positive to negative. For the HICs, the share of non-concessional loans more than doubled, DPI increased more than sevenfold and ODA increased by almost fourfold over the period 1980 to 1986. After 1986, aggregate resource flows declined dramatically. The pattern for SSA is considerably different. DPI has remained negligible here; the share of non-concessional loans has remained constant; the share of ODA has increased and the outflow of other capital has more than doubled. Since 1986, aggregate net resource flows have stabilised at about $10 bn per year and the ODA share of this has stabilised at 70%.

In this Chapter, we have looked at the current state of affairs in third world debt, the relative economic performance of the 15 HICs and the SSA group of countries and we have outlined the composition of debt in the Third World. Progress on debt and debt service reduction has given rise to some optimism over the past years in terms of alleviating the problem of Third World debt. However, debt and debt service agreements have been extended to only a few countries so far and so their impact on the debt and debt service indicators may be expected to be limited. Some external liabilities of the developing countries have declined but, as in the past, the situation differs markedly across regions with that of SSA continuing to rise and that of the HICs falling. However the fact that real GDP per capita continued to fall in both areas cements fears for the economic stability of these countries.

Footnotes

1 The definition of developing countries used here and throughout this analysis unless otherwise specified is that used by the IMF. Under the IMF classification scheme, the industrial countries comprise: Australia, Austria, Belgium, Canada, Denmark, Finland, France, Germany, Iceland, Ireland, Italy, Japan, Luxembourg, Netherlands, New Zealand, Norway, Spain, Sweden, Switzerland, United Kingdom and United States. Of these, the seven largest countries in terms of GNP – Canada, France, Germany, Italy, Japan, United Kingdom and United States – constitute the major industrial countries. All other country members of the IMF and "certain essentially autonomous dependent territories for which adequate statistics are available" (IMF *World Economic Outlook*, 1988, p. 103) fall into the category of Developing Countries.

2 When the money value of GDP is adjusted for changes in prices the resulting concept is called real GDP. It is a measure of the physical amount of goods and services produced domestically.

3 The IMF group of 15 heavily indebted countries includes: Argentina, Bolivia, Brazil, Chile, Colombia, Cote d'Ivoire, Ecuador, Mexico, Morocco, Nigeria, Peru, Philippines, Uruguay, Venezuela and Yugoslavia. To this group, the World Bank has added Costa Rica and Jamaica to make up its highly indebted countries group. This group of countries accounts for almost half of all developing countries' debt. Sub-Saharan Africa comprises all African countries and island-states (as defined by the IMF) south of the Sahara excluding South Africa. The excluded African countries are (usually): Algeria, Egypt, Libya, Morocco, South Africa, Tunisia and Western Sahara. In some cases, Nigeria is also excluded from this list.

4 The middle-income countries include Angola, the Congo, Cuba, the Dominican Republic, Egypt, Hungary, Iraq, Jordan, the Lebanon, Nicaragua, Poland and Syria. The low-income countries include Afghanistan, Burma, Cambodia, Guyana, Haiti, Laos, Mozambique, Pakistan, Sri Lanka and Vietnam.

5 Official creditors' international organisations such as the World Bank, the regional development banks, multilateral and intergovernmental agencies, governments and their agencies.

6 It is also likely that the World Bank figure considerably underestimates the true debt burden of Sub-Saharan Africa. See Green and Griffith-Jones (1986).

7 Traditionally, IMF adjustment programmes have involved the following policies: trade and financial flow liberalisation, an anti-inflation policy and a devaluation of the domestic currency. The first policy is relevant here. Liberalisation of trade and financial flows involves the reduction or abolition of import controls and controls on the movement of foreign exchange. These latter controls had usually been used by developing countries in an attempt to stem the country's loss of foreign exchange reserves through payments for imports, repatriation of profits abroad by foreign-owned companies and investment of funds abroad by domestic residents.

8 The Paris Club is an informal grouping of government representatives (from treasuries and foreign ministries) which meets to renegotiate debts owed to official bilateral creditors.

9 International organisations include the international agencies of the EU, the IMF, the OECD, OPEC, the Regional Development Banks, the UN, the World Bank and intergovernmental agencies which provide loans and credits to developing countries.

10 This includes banks as well as other financial institutions.

11 This covers sources of private credit other than banks, including manufacturers, exporters and other suppliers of goods.

12 This table is based on a sample of ninety developing countries.

Chapter 3

The Costs of the Debt Crisis

Introduction

Much of the literature which purports to discuss the "costs" of the debt crisis has focused on the more or less overt financial costs faced by Western banks, international financial institutions and the governments of the debtor and creditor countries. Indeed, it was the threat to the international financial system and the potential costs that this would entail which brought the issue of the Third World debt crisis to the forefront in 1982. More recently, some researchers (see for example UNICEF, 1987) have highlighted the costs of the crisis for the poorer members of the population of the debtor countries. In this Chapter, we consider the nature of the costs of adjustment to the debt crisis, who bears these costs and how they are and may be assessed. Given the bias of the literature, we have chosen to devote much of the analysis below to the costs of the debt crisis for the developing countries. As in the previous chapter, we focus largely on the 1980s as this is the period where the record is best documented.

In order to put the assessment of costs which follows below into perspective, we begin by providing a short summary of the development of the analytical framework for assessing the costs of adjustment from the standpoint of economics. In the 1950s, when maximisation of aggregate economic growth was the main objective of economic development, the growth rate of GNP or GNP per capita became the standard measure for assessing changes in the welfare of the population of an economy. Gradually, however, it became clear that higher GNP per capita did not necessarily result in higher incomes for each member of society – the benefits of growth did not always "trickle down". This led in the 1970s to the supplementation of GNP growth by measures of income distribution, income inequality and poverty in order to evaluate the effects of economic changes on the economic well-being or welfare of society. This shift in emphasis from the aggregate towards the micro level led development economists to study employment, unemployment and earnings structures in individual labour markets as well as the distribution of productive activities and other disaggregate phenomena. Then came the realisation that income need not be the sole measure of economic welfare. Indicators of the levels of basic human services and needs were developed. These include indicators of health, nutrition, education and shelter. A problem with such indicators is that it is difficult to combine all of the information in order to produce a single index of well-being. Attempts which have been made to do this – for example, the Overseas Development Council's (ODC) Physical Quality of Life Index[1] and the UNDP's Human Development Index[2] – produce interesting but not always intuitively appealing country rankings. We shall discuss these indexes in more depth below. We now turn our attention to an analysis of the nature and the costs of adjustment to the debt crisis.

Adjustment policies and aggregate costs

The point of departure here is 1982, following the recognition of the debt problem as a problem of international proportions. This is important since it means that we should be aware that some of the costs result from adjustment to the global recession of this period while other costs may be attributed to policies which were put in place in an attempt to alleviate the debt crisis. Unfortunately, it is not always possible to distinguish between the two sources of the costs. We do not attempt to do this here. Rather, we provide an outline of the costs of adjustment as perceived in the literature. Adjustment in the current context refers to the process of reacting to imbalances in a country's economy. Such imbalances may manifest themselves in a number of ways. In this case the reduction in foreign lending to the developing countries after August 1982 led to balance of payments deficits whose elimination was usually effected by the adoption of economic policies which would reduce a country's expenditures on imports and/or expand its export revenues. Many (but not all) of these measures involved changes in the structure of the economy, hence the name structural adjustment policies. We shall discuss these policies further below.

Between 1981 and 1983 external financing to all developing countries fell by approximately 40%. Over the same period, debt-related net transfers[3] changed from a positive value of $6.4 billion to a negative value of $2.4 billion – a downward trend continued thereafter.

The current account deficit on the BOP stood at $50.8 billion for the 15 HICs and $8.2 billion for Sub-Saharan Africa in 1982. These figures had fallen to $0.2 billion and $3.3 billion respectively by 1985. These changes were achieved mainly by turning trade balances from deficits to large surpluses. For example, the trade balance of the HICs went from a deficit of $7.5 billion in 1981 to a surplus of $41 billion by 1985, while the corresponding figures for SSA were $5.2 billion and $0.8 billion respectively. In the face of falling export prices for Third World products, improved trade balances were effected by drastically cutting import expenditures.

Which policies were used to achieve such turnarounds? It is useful here to refer to the distinction made between macroeconomic stabilisation and structural adjustment policies. The current account deficit may be viewed as an imbalance between aggregate demand and aggregate supply in the economy. Policies to restore balance may be classified into short-run macroeconomic or aggregate demand management policies and long-run resource reallocation policies which are aimed at putting the economy on a growth path. The former type of policies was predominant during the emergency phase of adjustment to the debt crisis (1982-85) while the latter has prevailed since the Baker Plan's emphasis on "adjustment with growth". Given the immediate objective in 1982 of reversing the (negative) flow of net resource transfers, most debtor countries responded by adopting short-run policies designed to reduce aggregate expenditures as well as policies designed to switch expenditures from foreign to domestic goods and services. For the most part, the choice of policies was based on the perception of their potential to restore the current account balance rapidly in the short-run as well as their consistency with promoting other objectives such as reducing inflation. Little or no attention was given to the implications of such policies for income distribution or welfare. Although many developing countries operated stabilisation and structural adjustment programmes under their own initiative, most debtor countries have put such programmes into place with IMF assistance. In the period 1980-85, an average of 47 developing countries had IMF-assisted programmes in operation each year.

Expenditure reduction policies are policies which aim to curtail the level of aggregate demand in the economy. They include restrictive domestic credit, fiscal and monetary policies, wage controls, real exchange rate devaluation and trade restrictions. While such policies are effective in restoring external balance (BOP current account), they generally do so at the expense of internal balance, i.e. lower output, income, employment and capacity utilisation in the domestic economy. Expenditure reducing policies in most debtor countries have focused on attempts to reduce public expenditure, in particular public investment expenditures and the wage bill of public sector employees. Restrictive monetary policy led to higher interest rates and reduced investment expenditures (Table 3.1). This meant reduced future income for the economy while the reduction in aggregate demand led to reduced output, employment and consumption (Table 3.1). The problem with the initial response to reduce public expenditure was that much foreign debt in developing countries is owed by the government. Real exchange rate devaluation raised the domestic currency costs of foreign payments and therefore increased the interest payments bill. This was financed for the most part by domestic credit creation which in turn led to inflation and even higher fiscal deficits (Table 3.1).

Expenditure switching policies aim to shift productive resources (labour and capital) from non-tradeable to tradeable goods and services and demand away from imports to domestically produced tradeable and non-tradeable goods and services – without changing total expenditure and thus leaving the internal balance unaffected. They have included exchange rate devaluations and trade restrictions, both quantitative (in the form of quotas and capital controls) and qualitative (tariffs), taxes, pricing strategies and encouragement of factor mobility. Exchange rate devaluations have led to rising price levels while quantitative trade restrictions have had, in some countries, the negative effect of cutting off supplies of some intermediate inputs which were essential for indigenous industries.

Structural adjustment policies, as considered necessary by the IMF for stabilisation and economic growth, include policies of trade liberalisation (varying in intensity from relaxation of trade and exchange controls to the complete elimination of quantitative restrictions and tariffs), reform of the financial system, exchange rate devaluation and reduction of the role of the state in the economy (for example, privatisation and fiscal reform). The objectives of such policies are improvement of the current account and balance of payments, lower fiscal deficits and reduced inflation. It is as yet somewhat premature to discuss the full effects and costs of such policies since they are by nature long-term policies.

Table 3.1: Gross capital formation (GCF) as % of GDP, annual rate of change (%) of GDP and GDP per capita, central government fiscal balances (CGFB) as % of GDP and annual rate of change (%) in consumer prices (INF): 15 HICs and Sub-Saharan Africa, 1983-89

	1983	1984	1985	1986	1987	1988	1989
GCF (% of GDP)							
15 HICs	17.7	16.1	16.8	17.5	18.9	19.7	18.6
Sub-Saharan Africa	17.1	17.3	18.4	18.4	18.7	18.0	17.6
Annual changes (%)							
Real GDP:							
15 HICs	-2.9	2.0	3.8	4.0	2.5	0.7	1.3
Sub-Saharan Africa	-0.2	1.1	3.9	3.9	1.6	2.2	1.9
Real GDP %:							
15 HICs	-4.9	-0.3	1.6	1.9	0.4	-1.4	-0.7
Sub-Saharan Africa	-3.1	-1.5	1.1	1.0	-1.2	-0.7	-1.0
CGFB (% of GDP)							
15 HICs	-5.6	-4.3	-5.9	-8.2	-9.1	-9.0	-11.9
Sub-Saharan Africa	-5.8	-5.1	-5.4	-6.1	-7.7	-7.1	-6.9
INF (%)							
15 HICs	90.9	118.4	122.7	77.4	116.6	248.6	480.7
Sub-Saharan Africa	25.6	21.6	19.8	20.5	23.1	21.7	19.6

Source: IMF World Economic Outlook, May 1990

Adjustment costs and their measurement

We begin by looking at the costs associated with the indirect effects and then turn our attention to those related to the direct effects, a distinction made by Cornia (1987b). The indirect effects are those which result from the effects of the adjustment policies on economic growth, income distribution and the extent of poverty in the economy. The direct effects are those which affect the level of well-being in the economy independently of the latter.

Indirect Effects/Costs: We have already seen that, at the aggregate level, one of the effects of expenditure reducing policies was reduced output and a slowdown in investment in the early years of the crisis, as illustrated in Table 3.1 above. It is also clear from this Table that real output per head fell between 1982 and 1989 in developing countries with the exception of 1985-87. How does this translate in costs at a more disaggregate level? We look first at indicators of income distribution. In theory, a distinction is made between the functional distribution of income (the division of income between the factors of production, viz. land, labour and capital) and the size distribution of income (based on its division among families and individuals). Since ownership of factors of production is a crucial determinant of income distribution, it would appear that the functional definition would prove to be a suitable concept for measuring income distribution and welfare. However, since the informal sector tends to be large in developing countries, this poses a major problem with the use of this definition. On the other hand, there are also many problems involved with relying on data on the size distribution of income in developing countries. These data generally come from sample surveys of households, following procedures perfected in the industrialised economies. However, economic structures differ vastly between industrialised and less developed countries as well as among the latter. Survey respondents may not know what their own/household income level is or they may for some reason under-report it. Earnings in developing countries in particular are prone to fluctuate greatly from year-to-year because of their sensitivity to the vagaries of nature, the market and/or political instability. For these reasons, it is essential to supplement measures of income distribution /inequality in developing countries with information drawn from a monitoring of other variables, such as food prices, real wage rates and public expenditure. We shall discuss these variables further below. With these caveats in mind, it is difficult to arrive at any clear-cut conclusion on the distributional effects/costs of adjustment policies.

Killick (1984) and the IMF (1986), on reviewing the empirical results, find no conclusive evidence that IMF programmes led to a systematic worsening of the income distribution in developing countries. Many of the empirical studies, in addition to looking at the size distribution of income, also report the Gini Concentration Ratio (GCR). The GCR provides a measure of equality in the distribution of income, with a theoretical range from zero (perfect equality) to one (perfect inequality). Cornia et al. (UNICEF, 1987) carried out an extensive analysis of the effects of adjustment policies in 10 developing countries (Botswana, Brazil, Chile, Ghana, Jamaica, Peru, Philippines, South Korea, Sri Lanka and Zimbabwe). Cornia found that, in 6 (Brazil, Chile, Peru, Philippines, South Korea and Sri Lanka) of the 10 countries studied for which data on income were available, income concentration increased. Cornia (1987b) goes on to state that the general conclusion in the literature from analysis of such measures is that there is no evidence of a worsening of income distribution as a result of measures taken to alleviate the debt crisis, except in Latin American countries.

Another way of assessing the indirect costs of adjustment policies is to consider their effect on the extent of poverty in the economy. The concept of income inequality relates to relative incomes while that of poverty evokes some notion of poor in an absolute sense. How is this measured? For the most part, the concept of the poverty line is used. This consists of defining a reference level of household income per capita, which is considered to be necessary to achieve a minimum acceptable standard of living. The simplest measure of the extent of poverty is then the percentage of the economy's households with incomes below this reference level. Of course, given differences between countries in what is perceived to be the minimum, this gives rise to a relative poverty line which differs across countries rather than some standardised global concept of absolute poverty. Cornia (1987b) finds evidence of an increase in the number of people below a given poverty line in Chile, Ghana, Jamaica, Peru and the Philippines. For example, in the rural areas of Ghana, the percentage of the population in poverty increased from 60-65% in 1974 to 70-75% in 1984. The general impression given in the literature from an analysis of such measures is that aggregate poverty in most debtor developing economies increased during the 1980s. As stressed above, however, there is no way of allocating the responsibility for this deterioration between general recession and adjustment to debt.

Direct Effects/Costs: Given the unreliability (and sometimes the unavailability) of income data in most developing countries, it is necessary to look at other variables in order to assess the effects/costs of adjustment policies on the well-being of the population. These variables include those which measure the direct costs of adjustment, such as reductions in government expenditure on health and education, increases in food prices and reductions in real food subsidies and regressive fiscal policies.

Real government expenditure per capita fell in more than 50% of the countries of the developing world between 1980-84. The greater proportion of this reduction occurred in countries with adjustment programmes, with per capita expenditures on health and education services being particularly badly hit. Data from the World Health Organisation (WHO) 1986 revealed a decline in public expenditure on health per capita in 14 out of 23 countries in Latin America between 1980 and 1984. Although reliable data are difficult to find, similar trends have been noted in the developing countries of Africa and Asia. Pinstrup-Andersen et al. (1987) present data for 23 developing countries with severe cuts in health and education expenditures. They find that declining GDP was associated with more severe cuts on health and education expenditures in Latin America than in Africa. On average, African countries tended to cut health expenditures more, while Latin American countries cut education expenditures more.

We saw in Table 3.1 that inflation figures of 3 digits were rampant throughout most of the 1980s in the HICs. Since many developing countries were at the same time pursuing policies of wage control, real wages have fallen. This decline is even more dramatic if the index of food prices rather than the CPI is used to calculate the real wage. The index of food prices is more appropriate in assessing the cost to the poorer sections of society than if it refers to the standard basket of goods purchased by the poor. Another factor which resulted in an increase in the real cost of living of the poor in developing countries is the decline in the real value of food subsidies which has occurred in many developing countries. This has not always been the result of a conscious policy to cut government expenditures in this area. In some cases it is the outcome of devaluations of the exchange rate and falls in the import prices of subsidised goods. Other fiscal policies which may be have a regressive impact include indirect taxes and tariffs. The IMF (1986) noted that of the programmes which it supported between 1980 and 1983, 76% involved increases in indirect taxes while 46% contained tariff increases.

Basic human needs indicators: These correspond broadly to the outcome indicators of Cornia et al. as distinct from the measures discussed above which might be classified as input indicators.[4] Outcome indicators reflect an attempt to measure the changes in well-being which result from changes in the input indicators. They are designed to indicate the extent to which basic human needs are being met in the economy. They include the infant mortality rate, the child death rate, the prevalence of disease, life expectancy at birth, the levels of nutrition intake and educational attainment. In 1987, the infant mortality rate was 117 per 1,000 live births and the primary school enrolment rate in 1988 were 66% of school-age children, as compared to 58% and 100% in the HICs. Cornia reports that Sub-Saharan Africa appears to be the most severely hit developing region in terms of rising infant and child mortality rates, increased malnutrition and a worsening in the level of educational attainment.

As noted above, one of the problems with such social indicators is how to combine them to get an overall picture of the level of well-being of a society. The ODC's physical quality of life index (PQLI) is an unweighted average of three indicators – the infant mortality rate, life expectancy at age one and the adult literacy rate – with each indicator being given a value between 0 and 100. The UNDP's human development index (HDI) is an average of scaled indexes of life expectancy at birth, adult literacy and real GDP per capita. Both indicators are subjective and give rise to some unusual rankings of countries. Using one year's HDI, Argentina is ranked four places above Portugal while in the class of developed economies, the US is ranked two places below Ireland. Clearly, there is no fool-proof way of constructing a non-arbitrary index. Any index of well-being and changes therein will inevitably depend on what socioeconomic indicators are taken into account and what weights are given to each one in the construction of the index. Such weights reflect the evaluator's values and the values of others are likely to diverge. Consensus is possible only in the broad sense that most observers would regard rising income per head, no worsening of income/wealth inequality, reduced poverty, and improved health and education as welfare improving.

Notwithstanding the point made in the last paragraph, the evidence reviewed in this Chapter – falling output and output per capita in most developing countries, mixed evidence on changes in income distribution, increasing percentages of populations in poverty, and the deterioration of many basic human needs indicators – it seems clear that human conditions deteriorated in the developing world in the 1980s. It is not possible, however, to allocate responsibility for this deterioration between debt-adjustment policies and responses to world-wide recession.

Footnote

1 Morris (1979)

2 *The Economist* (1990)

3 These are flows and transfers on account of all debt. They are defined by the World Bank as net disbursements on short- and long-term loans, and IMF credit minus interest payments on short and long-term loans and IMF charges.

4 The authors also distinguish process indicators which are designed to measure such things as food availability and access to education and health services.

Chapter 4

Plans and Initiatives

Introduction

The nature of the external debt problem for developing countries has been outlined in Part I. In the second part of the study we will examine how the various parties to the problem have responded. This will be done at two levels. First, we will outline the nature of the solutions that have been proposed. Second we will survey a sample of opinion concerning the approach to dealing with the debt problem.

The objective of this Chapter is to synthesise the proposals, which have been put forward since 1982, to alleviate the debt problem. It is by no means intended to be a comprehensive review of *all* the proposals. Rather, the objective is to outline the salient features of some major proposals within a cohesive framework.

In the second section we present the proposals within a typological framework. This framework is the same as that used by Feldstein et al (1987). Under their grouping scheme, proposals are classified under the following headings: procedural reforms; altering the nature of claims; altering the ownership of claims; and altering the value of claims.

This classification is not inviolable. For instance, certain proposals to alter the nature of claims could give rise to a reduction in the value of claims. In such situations we have been guided by the original intent of a particular scheme in deciding on the appropriate heading.

The original response from industrial countries to the debt problem involved a strategy of "muddling through". From 1985 this strategy gave way to concerted initiatives. We define an initiative as an attempt to implement a proposal or set of proposals. In regard to initiatives, a distinction must be drawn between middle-income and low-income debtors. The initiatives sponsored by US Treasury Secretaries Baker and Brady are principally of relevance to middle-income debtors that are concentrated in Latin America and who have large obligations to commercial banks. The low-income problem debtors are comprised mainly of Sub-Saharan African countries. Their debt obligations are mainly to official sources. The terms which emerged from the 1988 Toronto Summit of the Group of Seven industrial countries make up the most comprehensive debt alleviation initiative for this group. These initiatives are discussed on page 58ff.

Before proceeding we must note that the success of any scheme for debt alleviation will be influenced by the state of the world macroeconomy, the existence of protectionism, and capital flight from debtor countries. According to Dornbusch, "... the prospects of strong growth in the industrialised countries, lower interest rates, a weaker dollar and stronger real commodity prices were the central scenario which encouraged the 'muddling through process'..." in 1982.[1] While such a scenario is desirable, it is no longer considered to be a feasible plank on which to construct a solution to the debt problem. Consequently we do not devote space to a discussion of appropriate macro policies for industrialised countries.

An end to the crisis for debtors requires an easing of the foreign exchange constraint. Increased export volumes can go some way towards achieving this end. Protectionism in the US as a result of panic over trade deficits and in Europe through the adoption of a "fortress" stance following the internal liberalisation in 1992 would seriously jeopardise the debtors' attempts to adjust under any plan. The GATT and the Lomé process are central to avoiding this outcome. A discussion of these matters would go beyond the scope of this study, however.

The problem of capital flight relates to the large stock of debtor country (mainly Latin American) assets held in industrialised countries. If these assets were available to pay government guaranteed debts some of the Latin American countries would actually be net creditors! It is naive to imagine that a solution of this nature is feasible. Capital flight cannot be ignored, however. Steps can be taken which would make capital withdrawals from debtors more difficult. We postpone to Chapter 7 a more detailed discussion of this issue.

Typology of proposals

In this section the proposals will be explained and classified. We will present some critical commentary on the plans. Additional commentary in the context of criteria of equity will be contained in Chapter 7.

Procedural reform proposals

Plans under this heading seek to alter technical financial procedures related to the debt, without changing the expected payments of the debtor countries or reducing their burden of adjustment. They maintain the relationship between the original creditor and debtor while altering the details of the relationship. The impetus to devise such schemes derives from a recognition of the possibility that the debtor may repudiate or that default may be declared by the creditor. The objective is to avoid either of these extremes by making alterations in the details of the financial package. Such plans include multiyear rescheduling of the debt, conversion of debt to longer maturities and the development of insurance for the debt.

Procedural reform proposals involve some form of refinancing or rescheduling of debts. Such rescheduling "... is at once an admission of debt-servicing breakdown and a remedial measure for re-establishing more normal financial conditions".[2] It can therefore be thought of as financial engineering. There has been considerable innovation in the techniques adopted since the onset of the debt crisis. Some of the innovation has come about through learning from experience. However, changing perceptions have also been important. Regling (1988) argues that the initial financial packages in 1982/83 were based on the notion that the servicing problems of debtors was temporary. By the mid-1980s the longer term nature of the problem became apparent. This period saw the development of schemes that allowed banks to adjust their operations so as to maximise their benefits in the context of their domestic tax and regulatory environments. The schemes also facilitated the banks in withdrawing from lending to developing countries – total annual bank lending fell from $45 billion in 1982/83 to $11 billion in 1984/85 (Regling, 1988). From the debtors' perspective, relief came in the form of longer-term refinancing arrangements. By 1987, positive net transfers from debtors and difficulties in reaching agreements gave rise to a search for new techniques.

The scope of plans under this heading and the next must be

seen in the limited context of financial engineering. However, any solution to the debt problem will, by definition, involve financial engineering. Hence, experience with the schemes described here may suggest their usefulness in a broader context than that in which they were originally conceived.

Rescheduling

Renegotiation of the terms of debt contracts typically takes place collectively at informal routine meetings called clubs. Negotiations with private creditors take place at the London Club or the New York Club while official creditors meet at the Paris Club. Both parties to a debt contract have an incentive to reschedule. For lenders rescheduling is preferable to default as there remains some possibility of recovering the full value of the loan. The incentive for debtors to participate in rescheduling rather than to repudiate arises from fear of trade impediments or seizure of assets.

The *nature* of debt rescheduling is best explained with the aid of an example. Imagine that a loan is taken out which is to be repaid over ten years. Each year the payments on the loan will include interest and amortization (i.e. repayment of principle). The loan contract will also specify the timing of payments. We will set this detail aside for the moment. In year two the debtor finds that she has difficulty in making payment. The bank offers to reschedule the amortization profile. In addition they offer her a grace period of two years. This involves consolidating the principal payments for year two and adding them to principal payments from year five onwards. In return for this service the bank will charge her a fee and/or put her in a higher interest bracket.

An illustration of the possible effect of rescheduling on a country's amortization profile is Brazil. The revised schedule was devised on the assumption that Brazil would reschedule $5.5 billion in long-term bank debt coming due in 1984 and $2 billion to official creditors. The example is due to Cline (1984). The actual profile that emerged subsequently differed on account of later changes. Nevertheless we get an idea of the way that rescheduling can ease temporary difficulties for a debtor while compensating the creditor.

The precursor to major rescheduling was the rescue packages orchestrated by the IMF and Western governments for Argentina, Brazil, Mexico and Yugoslavia in the wake of the crisis atmosphere of 1982.[3] Mexico received trade credits and prepayment for oil from the US. Yugoslavia also received trade credits from the US and other governments. Brazil received an emergency loan from the US. Each of the countries received bridging loans from Western central banks via the Bank for International Settlements. These schemes allowed a breathing space for the countries to negotiate terms with the IMF.

At this point the IMF changed tactics. Previously they had been content to leave their provision of stand-by lending act as a signal to banks to resume lending. Now ".. they [the IMF] explicitly told the private banks that if they did not provide new lending themselves there would be no new IMF money whatsoever".[4] This forced the banks to extend new loans. Cline also believes that it helped to alleviate a "free-rider" problem, i.e., a situation where small banks benefit from an improvement in the quality of their loans because of increased lending by large banks while at the same time not extending any new loans themselves. This was the scenario from which new forms of rescheduling developed.

Multi-year rescheduling

Prior to the debt crisis the consolidation period for rescheduling normally extended to no more than a year and then only for that portion of debt immediately due. This was referred to as the "short-leash" norm. Regular contact with the debtors over their loan terms was perceived to be important by creditors. This procedure continued up to 1984. In June 1984, the concept of a multi-year rescheduling agreement (MYRA) for those countries who had successfully undertaken economic adjustment prog-rammes was endorsed for the first time at the London summit of leaders of seven advanced capitalist countries. The essence of a MYRA is that it looks ahead and reschedules debt falling due in future peak years. This is important in the following context. In the aftermath of the second oil shock, many countries increased their debts substantially during 1980-82. Much of this debt was medium-term with a maturity of 5-7 years. This resulted in a bunching of principal repayments in the mid to late 1980's. Given the shortage of foreign exchange income in many indebted countries, there was widespread recognition that it would be impracticable to expect that such countries would be able to service their amortization in the mid to late 1980's. In the absence of new financial flows to these countries, it was inevitable that there would have to be some form of rescheduling of the debt.

The shift to multi-year rescheduling does not change the total value of debt to the debtor. Rather, the risk of crisis is reduced through increasing the flexibility of technical factors associated with debt structure.

The first country to take this initiative was Mexico in 1984. In September 1984, Mexico negotiated an agreement that debt falling due during 1985-90 would be rescheduled over 14 years. This was supported by both Jaques de Larosiere, then Director of the IMF, and by Paul Volcker, then Chairman of the US Federal Reserve System. Other Latin American countries followed Mexico's example. In most cases, the achievement of a MYRA required that the country be in good standing with the IMF. Reschedulings of official debt also took place through the Paris Club. For example, Sudan, in 1983 and 1984, obtained a debt rescheduling covering 100% of debt due in 1983-84, with grace periods of over 6 years and a total maturity of 16 years.

We mentioned above that the banks charge for rescheduling. Initially the charge for developing country debt involved a fee and an increase in the interest rate spread. The base from which to calculate the spread was also changed from LIBOR to the US prime rate, at the time three-quarters of a percentage point higher on average. These charges gave rise to considerable disquiet. Cline (1984) estimated that Mexico's 1983 rescheduling agreement would increase annual interest payments by about $560 million. This is excluding the rescheduling fee and higher interest rates on new loans.

The size of interest rate spreads was the subject of considerable debate. Higher spreads were considered necessary: to compensate the banks for higher risk; to discourage unnecessary rescheduling; and to act as an incentive for banks to continue lending. The last point is not very convincing since the larger banks were locked in what was known as "involuntary lending" – a lender's trap whereby they must extend more money in order to preserve the quality of earlier loans.

The question then is whether the large spreads represented the market price of risk and "discouragement" suggests that there is no "natural market price": the actual price that emerges depends on relative bargaining strengths.[5] This point reoccurs often in discussion of solutions to the debt problem. In this specific case Cline suggested that spreads be reduced to convey a sense of equity in the process to debtor countries.

Further development of rescheduling

Subsequent developments in rescheduling involved the use of: interest rate options; currency redenomination of loans; and alterations in interest rate timing (Regling, 1988). With currency redenomination banks are afforded an asset management technique which alows them to diversify against exchange rate risk. Existing loans can be redenominated or new loans can be denominated in a bank's domestic currency once the currency is internationally convertible. The currency denomination of the loan is a one time choice which must be made at the time the debt becomes subject to the refinancing agreement. For debtor countries a benefit may acrue if the redenomination is to a currency with a lower interest rate.[6] This option was built into restructuring agreements concluded with nine countries – Argentina, Brazil, Chile, Mexico, Mozambique, Nigeria, the Philippines, Uruguay, and Venezuela – in 1986/87.

Interest rate options concern the base on which spreads are calculated or the option to convert to a fixed rate. By the late 1980s the US prime rate was excluded as a base option for most agreements because on average it was higher than the LIBOR. The choice of base gave flexibility to banks. The conversion to fixed rates was used in conjunction with the currency redenomination option. This saw debts being converted to low interest currencies such as the Yen and Deutsche Mark at fixed interest rates.

It was noted earlier that a loan contract involved not only a scheduling of payments but also a specific timing. In a small number of cases – Argentina in 1987 and Chile in 1985 and 1987 – rescheduling has involved the retiming of interest payments. The debtor is given temporary breathing space at the cost of longer term interest rates. Banks can extend finance in this way without increasing their exposure through the committment of new money.

Some proposals for debt reform have called for the stretchout of debt to longer maturities. This is basically another form of debt rescheduling, designed to alleviate the problem of bunching of principal repayments described above. In fact, the 1984 MYRA package for Mexico, which was mentioned above, included new lending of $3.8 billion with an extended maturity of ten years.

Since proposals for the lengthening of loan maturities have generally formed part of more broad-based proposals which are discussed in more detail below, reference to such proposals here will be brief. Felix Rohatyn (1983), financier,[7] put forward a proposal which included the stretching out of the debt of developing countries to long-term maturities of 15-30 years. This conversion would be carried out by the IMF or the World Bank or a totally new international agency. This agency would buy the claims of the banks through its own issue of long-term bonds. Rohatyn believed that this longer-maturity conversion of the debt would impose a loss on the banks. He saw the division of this loss among the stockholders of the banks, taxpayers and countries as an issue which would have to be resolved. He argued that any loss accruing to the banks would have to be balanced against the greater asset security that such a change would achieve. Stretch-out of maturities also formed part of proposals put forward by Kenen (1983), Schumer (1983) and Bradley (1986), which will be discussed later.

An extreme form of maturity lengthening is considered in a package of debt reform measures put forward by Professors Jack Gutentag and Richard Herring (1983) of the University of Pennsylvania. They suggest that countries in difficulty should be allowed to convert their existing debt to consols at market interest rates. This means that interest must be paid for ever but the principal is never repaid. This suggestion is an example of what Regling (1988) calls securitisation. An early example was the issue of promissory notes on a restricted basis in the 1983 Nigerian restructuring. Securitisation involves the substitution of tradeable financial instruments (which can be sold off by the creditors) for bank claims. As such the development of a secondary market for debt would be necessary for its widespread use. Secondary markets will be discussed below.

It is interesting to note that stretching-out of maturities was considered a red herring by Cline.[8] Since principal was being rescheduled and since roll over would continue once normal conditions were restored he saw no advantage in longer maturities. In other words he did not entertain the idea of reducing the face value of debt. He noted that interest payments constituted the major burden for debtors and that principal rescheduling would not alleviate this burden. Below we examine proposals to alter the flow of interest payments.

Risk reduction for creditors

A separate genre of proposals considers schemes to aid the banks in spreading the risks of their claims on developing country debtors through the insurance of their risks. Advocates of such risk-spreading policies generally argue that governments or official agencies need to act as market creators in these contexts because the problem of moral hazard prevents their development. "Moral hazard", in this context, refers to the possibility that the existence of insurance will induce changes in action by the insured (less care against preventing the occurrence of a bad state in which an insurance pay-out must be made) that will result in losses for the insurer. The argument for insurance is that the existence of such markets would, by spreading the risk of default by a particular country, serve to reduce the threat to an individual bank, which was heavily committed to Third World debt, of becoming insolvent, should such a default occur.

The idea of an insurance scheme aimed at facilitating relationships between the debtors and the creditors is not a novel one. Grubel (1979) advocated the setting up of an International Deposit Insurance Corporation, which would insure deposits around the world. The idea of insurance re-emerged in the early 1980's. Many proposals build on the existing mechanism of export credit by sponsoring new insurance schemes based on the existing official export credit agencies, while others envisage the creation of a new official insurance institution.

A number of proposals involve some sort of co-financing with an official agency as a means of reducing risk. Minos Zombanakis (1983), financier, proposed that existing sovereign debt should be rescheduled for up to thirteen years under the supervision of the IMF. If after ten years a country was unable to service its debt, despite adherence to the IMF programme, it would have its payments guaranteed by the IMF for the final three years.

Lord Harold Lever (Lever and Huhne, 1985), British ex-minister, proposed that the official export credit agencies of the industrial countries, acting jointly, should guarantee borrowing undertaken by countries to finance what is deemed by the IMF to be a reasonable balance of payments deficit. These guarantees would not be linked to exports from a particular country but rather to the agreed financing needs of the borrowing country. William Bolin, of Bank of America, and Jorge del Canto (1983), formerly of the IMF, put forward a similar proposal. They suggest that an export development fund (EDF) should be created. This would be backed by the export credit agencies of the industrialised countries and loosely linked to the World Bank and it would make long-term loans to developing countries for capital equipment imported from the industrial countries. These loans would be guaranteed by the EDF.

Johannes Witeveen (1983), former managing director of the IMF, advocated the creation of an IMF-administered facility, which would guarantee bank loans against political risks in the debtor countries. This guarantee would be available to commercial banks on condition that the debtors were in compliance with the IMF programme performance criteria. Professor Henry Wallich (1984), a member of the Board of Governors of the Federal Reserve System, discusses an insurance scheme which would cover the banks credit portfolio of assets rather than individual credits. The banks themselves would fund the insurance scheme. Any official financial contributions to the scheme by national and international institutions would have to be repaid at a later date.

The World Bank participated in a number of co-financing schemes between 1985 and 1987. In the cases of Chile and Mexico some parts of their lending packages carried World Bank guarantees (Regling, 1988). This type of arrangement became more important in 1989 as a consequence of the Brady initiative which is discussed later in this Chapter.

Gutentag and Herring argue against insurance schemes such as those described above, arguing that "insurance that is both comprehensive and complete presents enormous moral hazard".[9] They argue that insurance schemes encourage rather than restrain banks from becoming insolvent, since they know that they will be bailed out by the insuring agency's funds. They argue instead for the creation of secondary markets for debt by official institutions. Under this scheme banks could sell off loans at a market rate to the World Bank, the IMF or a new institution. The purchasing institution would combine these loans with similar loans of other banks and resell them to public participants in the market. The question of developing secondary markets for debt is taken up in the next subsection.

Altering the nature of claims on the debtor nations

The objective of proposals in this category is to curtail or eliminate the need for debtor countries to seek new loans by altering the nature of claims on them so as to achieve a schedule for debt service obligations which they can accommodate. The schemes outlined below typically involve the use of instruments which are expected to achieve the latter objective without reducing the value of the claims to creditors.

We will distinguish between three broad types of proposals under this heading. First we examine schemes that directly alter the flow of interest service. Next we will discuss the development of a secondary market for debt. Finally we consider schemes that seek to make repayments more flexible and/or sensitive to economic conditions.

Changing the flow of interest service

Interest capitalisation involves the banks adding part of their interest claims on developing country debt to the principal due on maturity of the debt. It is therefore a means by which debtors may defer their interest payments obligations. There was a certain amount of interest in this idea in the mid 1980s. For the debtors this proposal had the advantage of directly reducing the immediate resource transfer. Some banks, especially those in Europe, favoured this approach, because of tax incentives in their domestic countries. In addition it was thought to be useful in circumventing the "free-rider" problem whereby smaller banks attempted to opt out of "involuntary lending". Unlike new lending, capitalisation of interest payments does not require the approval of bank boards. Therefore smaller banks would be unable to use excuses relating to the attitude of their board as a means of not participating in schemes.

Capitalisation was opposed on a number of counts. In the first place US banks would face regulatory difficulties. When this scheme was raised it was pointed out that capitalisation, under US banking regulations, was tantamount to nonpayment: the loans involved would be declared non-performing.[10] Cline argued that capitalisation would have adverse stock market consequences that would make it difficult for banks to improve their capital base and would lead to instability in the financial structure.[11]

For debtors, it was argued that capitalisation would induce substantial net debt accumulation. This would result from the loss of influence by banks in the terms and conditions of restructuring. In the case of new loans disbursal takes place in quarterly increments. If the banks are unhappy with the course of economic policy in a debtor country they can suspend disbursements. This condition would be lost if debtors could decide unilateraly to capitalise interest payments. There has been very little formal capitalisation of interest payments: the only example since 1982 being Sudan's 1985 restructuring package.

"Interest capping" is a scheme which involves the application of a target interest rate. Two types of interest capping have been proposed – liquidity capping and concessional capping. Liquidity capping is intended to stabilise interest payments over time. A target interest rate is set for both new and rescheduled loans. If the market rate of interest rises above this target, the excess of interest payments due is added to the principal due on maturity of the loan. If the market interest rate falls below the target rate, repayments continue to be made at the target rate and the difference is deducted from the principal. Thus the relief offered to debtor countries by such a policy would depend on future movements in the real interest rate relative to the agreed target rate. While liquidity capping merely redistributes interest payments over time, a concessional interest cap usually involves forgiveness of interest payments and therefore does not increase the future debt burden. For that reason, we shall discuss concessional capping along with proposals for debt reduction.

Wallich (1983) included a proposal for interest capping, whereby any interest in excess of inflation plus a normal real interest rate would be capitalised. Massad and Zahler (1984), economists at the Economic Commission for Latin America (ECLA), advocate a variation of interest capping. They define a "reference" interest rate as the sum of the long-term average of real international interest rates and the average of spreads around this rate. National debtors pay the full amount of the market interest rate to their Central Bank. If the market interest rate is higher than the reference rate, the Central Bank pays the creditors at the reference rate and places the excess in an accumulating fund of the national currencies of the creditors. This fund is drawn upon when the market rate falls below the reference rate. The difference between this proposal and the interest liquidity cap discussed above is the existence of surplus funds in the national currencies, which is intended to provide a better basis for future repayments.

In 1988, Professor Rudiger Dornbusch of MIT proposed a scheme which he called "interest recycling". It involves an element of interest capitalisation but it is more broadly based. The emphasis of the scheme is on reconstruction in the debtor countries. His proposal is as follows: "[a]ctual [interest] payments in dollars would be reduced to the service of trade credit and possibly the loans of multilateral organisations. The remaining interest payments would in part be capitalised, thus freeing resources for much needed public sector investment, and in part they would be made in local currency. Creditors who receive the local currency payments could use them for unrestricted investment in the debtor countries' economies" (Dornbusch, 1988).

As a counterpart to the proposal Dornbusch suggested that debtor countries be obliged to introduce legislative reform to provide leeway for foreign direct investment and that they also undertake microeconomic reforms. Creditors would not be allowed to transfer abroad any payments made in local currencies. Claims to payment could, however, be sold. In this it would be like a debt-equity swap (to be discusssed below) applied to interest rather than principal.

In addition to the fact that the debtor countries face difficulties in acquiring sufficient foreign exchange to service their debts, there is the additional factor that actual interest payments made come mainly at the expense of domestic investment expenditure.

This was one of the issues that motivated Dornbusch's proposal discussed above. Another solution which has been proposed for this problem is the conversion of debt into investment. This involves the use of a secondary market for developing country debt.

Secondary market for debt

The secondary market developed initially to allow interbank swaps which had the purpose of consolidating portfolios and managing risk. The market developed rapidly from 1985 after Chile and Mexico introduced systematic debt conversion programmes. The growth of the market was based on swaps that involved the sale of claims at discount. Official sector backing for such market-based debt conversion schemes was important in the tenfold increase in the annual value of conversions between 1986 and 1988. By 1988 the annual value of conversions had reached $22 billion (World Bank, 1989).

The most common form of secondary market transaction has been the debt-equity swap,[12] whereby a bank's debt claim is converted into a foreign investor's equity holding. This involves a complex financial transaction which usually involves a foreign bank, a foreign investor, usually a multinational corporation, and the debtor country domestic authorities. The mechanics of the swap are illustrated by the following hypothetical example. Anybank of the US sells Mexican government bonds at a discount to Anycomp Inc. of the US. Anycomp Inc. presents the bonds to the Mexican monetary authorities for redemption in pesos. Anycomp Inc. invests this money in the Mexican economy (usually by purchasing a stake in a local firm) in a way which is agreed upon by Anycomp Inc. and the Mexican authorities. It appears, on first sight, that everyone gains. The bank disposes of some illiquid assets; the investing company gets pesos at a discount; and the debtor country can pay off the foreign debt in local rather than foreign currency, in addition to furthering investment in the domestic economy. The aspect of debt relief to the debtor country will be discussed in 'Altering the value of claims' on page 56. Of course the debtor country has to finance the purchase of the debt claim from the foreign investor. The domestic country government could raise the needed finance by selling its own bonds domestically and use the proceeds to buy back the foreign debt. If this happens, the effect is an exchange of foreign debt for domestic debt. Another side-effect is that the debtor country has ceded part of its ownership of capital stock to a foreign investor.

How does the debt-equity swap fit into the category of changing the nature of claims without reducing the amount of the debt to be paid off by the debtor? The nature of investment is usually such that dividend earnings to the investor might be expected to be small initially but to grow over time with inflation and a growing economy. This means that the debt-equity conversion may be seen as a stretch-out of repayments – dividend payments would be smaller than the interest repayments on the debt initially and larger at a later point in time. Hence, debt-equity swaps may be described in terms of a balance sheet operation rather than a resource transfer.

The main advocates of debt-equity swaps have been the banking institutions.[13] Initially debt-equity swaps were hyped to the extent that they were seen as the panacea for debt difficulties. This was unrealistic as Blackwell and Nocera point out. In their opinion "the limitations imposed by monetary fiscal and other economic considerations mean that the amount of debt-equity swaps that can be financed has to remain somewhat limited".[14] Figures from the World Bank suggest that the total value of debt conversions had fallen back to $14 billion in 1989. This was due in large part to the elimination of debt-equity programmes in Argentina, Brazil and Mexico which was in turn motivated by the adverse effects of the programmes on monetary expansion.[15] These effects arise because dividend payments were being made in domestic currency i.e., additional money was being printed, thus fuelling inflation. There have, however, been a shift to other forms of secondary market transaction which we will discuss below.

Increasing the flexibility of repayment

Finally in this category we will discuss proposals that involve the creation of instruments to increase repayment flexibility. One such scheme would be the expansion of the IMF's Compensatory Financing Facility (CFF). This facility was designed by the IMF to allow its members to borrow and repay funds in such a way as to smooth variations in its financial reserves caused by export earnings fluctuations and thereby to maintain its importing capacity.[16] A proposal in *The Economist* (1983) argued that the IMF's CFF should be extended to provide loans to offset variations in nominal interest payments.

An interesting proposal to change the nature of the claims on the debtor countries was put forward by Bailey, Luft and Robinson (1983) and Bailey (1983). They suggested that the existing fixed-interest claims should be replaced by shares in a country's exports called exchange participation notes (EPN).

These notes would be issued by the Central Banks of debtor countries to their creditors. In effect, they would entitle the commercial banks to a share of the foreign exchange earnings of the borrowing country. This means that a country's debt service payments would be linked to the country's foreign exchange earnings or ability to repay. In other words, the country's debt has been converted into an asset equity on the country's foreign exchange earnings capacity. Interest repayments are indexed to growth in the country's real exports.

The linking of interest service payments to some definition of ability to pay is not a new idea. Harvey (1981) advocated the introduction of "bisque clauses" into both new and old lending arrangements. These clauses would allow governments to postpone part of their service repayments, because of adverse economic conditions. The deferred payments could be made when economic conditions improved or when the original maturity of the loan was reached. A more explicit linking of debt service payments to ability to pay was contained in other proposals. For example, the Sistema Economico Latinoamericano (SELA) in 1984, suggested that a maximum of 20% of export earnings should be allocated to debt servicing. President Alan Garcia declared in July 1985 that Peru would limit its debt service to 10% of its export earnings. In 1986, Nigeria limited its repayments to 30% of its export receipts. The Cartagena Group advocated that external debt service payments should not absorb export earnings beyond "reasonable limits".

These proposals (with the exception of the more radical proposals outlined in the last paragraph) can essentially be thought of as contingent lending obligations. That is they are agreements by creditors to provide interest service relief if particular events occur. In general such an event could be a terms of trade decline, high world interest rates or export losses.

Altering the ownership of claims

The idea here is that a new official agency would be set up to act as an official intermediary between private creditors and developing countries in providing new lending to debtor countries or by assuming all the claims of private creditors on the developing countries. For analytical purposes such proposals may be separated into two groups. The first group encompasses those which propose that official institutions play an incremental role as suppliers of new loans to the debtor countries. The second group encompasses proposals that call for a complete take-over of the debt from the commercial banks in return for claims on the official institution.

Incremental official lender

George Soros (1984), a New York fund manager, in a very detailed proposal, suggested the formation of an International Lending Agency (ILA), which would act as a supplier of new credit to developing countries. Initially, the ILA's credit would be guaranteed by the industrial countries through a contingent allocation of special drawing rights by the IMF. The capital of the ILA would be built up by the contributions of present bank lenders and the contributions of debtor nations. In this way, the credit guarantee of the industrial countries could be phased out over time. The ILA would provide debtor nations with loans at long-term rates and maturities and a smoothed out interest arrangement. In the short-term, the ILA would play the role of an emergency facility by providing the necessary new credit to the debtor countries to make the interest payments on their outstanding debts. In this sense, the objective of the ILA is similar to the Lever proposal discussed above. In the long-term, the ILA would become a normal, self-sustaining, lending agency.

Following the same theme, Mahbub ul Haq (1984) proposed the setting up of a debt refinancing subsidiary (DRS) under the IMF. The purpose of the DRS would be to arrange new lending packages in the capacity of an intermediary between the lenders and the debtor countries. Another plan by Hervé de Carmoy (1987) considers the setting up of a fund to provide resources for eligible country borrowers, under the joint responsibility of the EU, the US and Japan. Finance would be provided by the governments of these countries, the World Bank, other multilateral development banks and the commercial banks. Resources from the fund would be made available to "eligible" debtor countries on condition that approved economic growth-promoting structural reform programmes would be adhered to by the borrower. An Action Committee, composed of officials of the public and private sectors of the participating industrial countries, would administer the fund with advice from the multilateral institutions.

Official takeover of debt

The two major proposals under this heading are those of Kenen (1983) and Rohatyn (1983), already referred to above. We note that most of the schemes discussed here involve debt discounting, a form of debt relief which will be discussed further in the next section.

Kenen (1983) called for the creation of a new international institution, the International Debt Discount Corporation

(IDDC), which would issue long-term bonds to banks in exchange for the debt of the developing countries. The arrangement would also have a debt forgiveness component since debts would be purchased at a discount of 10% of their book value. The debts of developing countries would be rescheduled by the IDDC on a one-time long-term basis: half of the earnings accruing to IDDC from the loans they have acquired would be used to provide debt relief in the form of lower interest rates or grace periods for repayment. Banks would be given a limited period of time to decide whether to participate in the scheme and the debtor countries would also be given an option to participate or not. Capital subscriptions for the IDDC would be provided by the governments of the industrial countries.

An update on this proposal is outlined in Kenen (1990). Among the points that should be noted are the following. The IDDC would only purchase debtor government guaranteed claims having an original maturity greater than one year. When the plan was originally unveiled there did not exist a broadly based secondary market for sovereign debt. Kenen recognises that the IDDC would need to take care to plan against appreciation of prices in the secondary market in anticipation of its creation. Creditor banks should not be allowed to sell some claims to the IDDC while retaining others. Sponsoring governments should also be required to alter banking regulations if this is necessary to facilitate banks dealing with the IDDC. In addition they should allow banks the option of gradually amortizing losses incurred by discounting debt with the IDDC. Finally claims transferred to the IDDC would be converted to long-term debt at a level slightly above the discounted value of the claims thus yielding a "profit" for the IDDC.

Rohatyn (1983) suggested a scheme whereby the banks' claims on the debtor countries would be converted into long-term (25-30 years), low-interest bonds (6%) issued by an existing (IMF or World Bank subsidiary) or new multilateral agency. The entity, guaranteed by the governments of the industrial countries, would acquire the banks' credit in return for its own bonds. Rohatyn envisaged that this scheme would involve a reduction of debt service payments to 25-30% of export earnings. Although the banks would lose out in terms of current and perhaps also in terms of capital write-off, Rohatyn felt that some of the losses should be absorbed by the industrial country governments.

A proposal in a similar vein to the two described above is that of Robinson (1988), chairman and chief executive officer of the American Express Company. He discusses the formation of an

Institute of International Debt and Development (I2D2), a joint venture of the IMF and the World Bank. Initial capital would be provided by the developed country governments. The Institute would purchase developing country loans from creditor banks at a discount and would pay for them by issuing its own floating rate consols or perpetual bonds. Participating debtor countries would have to pursue economic reform programmes, which would be negotiated on a case-by-case basis. Besides providing debt relief, the I2D2 would operate a policy of debt subordination. This means that all new loans issued by the Institute would have a prior claim on resources over existing debt purchased from the banks. As in the Rohatyn plan, this scheme would entail a loss for the banks.

Altering the value of claims

These proposals call for a reduction in creditor claims on developing countries – in short, outright debt relief or forgiveness at the creditors' expense. This category covers all proposals which involve debt relief, i.e. a reduction in the debt service obligations – both interest and principal – of the debtor countries at the expense of the creditors. Debt forgiveness involves a partial or a total write-off of developing country debt by the banks or other creditors.

Proposals for outright debt forgiveness, either total or partial, have grown in recent years. We have already seen that the proposals of Kenen (1983) and Rohatyn (1983) involved major elements of debt relief, which would be achieved mainly through the purchase of bank debt at a discount and its reorganisation on terms which would be more in line with the debtor's ability to pay. Dornbusch and Fischer (1984) proposed a reduction in the interest rates paid by developing countries over a short time period. The objective was to provide interest service relief in the short-run while limiting the loss incurred by the banks.

Calls for forgiveness have also come from politicians and debtor countries (ECLAC, 1986). Congressman Charles Schumer (1983), a New York Democrat, put forward a plan for conversion of bank loans to long-term, low-interest loans, under the guidance of the IMF. This plan also included an interest rate reduction for debtor countries facing repayment difficulties. Senator Bill Bradley (1986), a New Jersey Democrat, outlined a plan which calls for a reduction of three percentage points in interest rates, new lending and debt write-downs. He considers how the regulatory system should be adapted to facilitate write-downs agreed between debtors and creditors. He emphasises in particular the creation of a link between trade concessions by debtor countries and targeted, limited debt relief.

It is only recently, however, that proposals for outright debt relief have been discussed widely in official and political circles. During 1987 and 1988 the failure of the Baker initiative to restore growth in debtor countries and the general impasse in debt negotiations gave rise to discussions about outright forgiveness. In the next Chapter we survey more generally the shift of opinion towards forgiveness. By early 1989 the unveiling of the Brady initiative gave official backing to debt reduction.

The challenge then was to find the best method of granting debt reduction. The experience with financial engineering is useful for meeting this challenge. It would seem that there are two broad types of mechanism for introducing debt relief: the creation of a facility along the lines suggested by Kenen (1983 and 1990); or direct bargaining between a debtor and representatives of its creditor banks. The range of methods for financial engineering discussed earlier could be used under either approach. Basically this amounts to some sort of interest capping/capitalisation/recycling or resort to the secondary market. Of course, with the Kenen scheme the facility would dominate this market.

Schemes for facilitating debt repudiation

In anticipation of debt reduction, some new instruments have emerged in the secondary market. Principal among these are schemes to swap or "defease"[17] claims into exit bonds. The idea behind an exit bond is that it is a long-term bond with a low interest rate which allows the purchaser not to participate in any future rescheduling or concerted lending. In this sense it is the final exit for banks – a market means of getting out of involuntary lending. Thus, albeit at a cost, the banks avoid any further obligation to give debt relief. A number of variants on these bonds are possible. First they could involve a write-down of the face value of the debt and actually pay a higher interest rate than the previous claim. Second there is the question of backing for these bonds. In the case of the March 1988 Mexican defeasement scheme $2.5 billion dollars of debt was exchanged for bonds which were collaterised by Mexican purchases of US Treasury zero-coupon securities.[18] Without collateral, the bonds would require some seniority for payment in order to be attractive. Indeed Williamson (1988) argues that guarantees from the World Bank would be needed. It is interesting to note that this is exactly what the Brady initiative proposed.

The other option which emerged in 1988 was the notion of a debt buy-back. With a debt buy-back a country repurchases its debt at a discount. The obvious difficulty here is that funds must be available upfront. This raises the question as to whether donor governments would be happy to see earmarked aid re-routed to debt buy-backs. In addition it is not clear to what extent mandatory prepayment clauses in loan contracts preclude creditor banks from engaging in buy-backs.[19] Nevertheless Williamson believes that buy-backs will be easier to facilitate than exit bonds and he favours this route for bank exit. His proposal for debt reduction is a combination of this exit facility and sensitive interest capitalisation.

We have not discussed proposals involving debt default, moratorium and repudiation above. The reason is that such courses of action or the threat thereof represent more a response of individual countries to crisis situations (for example the temporary moratoria declared by Peru and Brazil in 1985 and Brazil in 1987) or a bargaining ploy in their negotiations rather than an integral part of any proposal to solve the debt crisis. In contrast to the 1930s where debt crisis negotiations followed default, such negotiations in the 1980s have sought to avoid default.

Initiatives

The Baker Plan

The Baker Plan marks a watershed for a number of reasons. It represents the beginning of the search for a "new solution" to the debt crisis. In 1985 debtor governments became more active in making proposals and in taking unilateral action. 1985 saw a deterioration in the international economic environment in the form of a slowdown of world trade growth, a further decline in commodity prices and a slowdown in net new lending by banks to debtor economies. Debtor countries saw their prospects for economic growth becoming more and more bleak. The Baker Plan is a proposal which reflects the concerns of debtor governments, the US and others, on the perceived drawbacks of existing methods of debt crisis management.

The Baker Plan was put forward by US Treasury Secretary James Baker III at the annual meeting of the World Bank and IMF in Seoul, South Korea, in October 1985. The objective of this plan was to promote "growth with adjustment", i.e. the pursuit of particular economic policies by the debtor countries which would promote economic growth and reduce their dependence on external finance. This proposal for overcoming the debt problems of the developing countries involved commitments by the debtor countries to pursue economic policies approved by the IMF and by the multilateral institutions and the commercial banks to provide additional lending. More specifically, the Baker Initiative contained two parts. The first, Baker I, was aimed at 15 heavily indebted middle income countries (Argentina, Bolivia, Brazil, Chile, Colombia, Cote d'Ivoire, Ecuador, Mexico, Morocco, Nigeria, Peru, Philippines, Uruguay, Venezuela and Yugoslavia) and contained 3 elements:

(1) The debtor country would adopt a set of macroeconomic and structural policies, which would encourage economic growth, reduce inflation and improve the balance of payments. Such policy changes would involve: tax and labour market reforms, development of financial markets, placing more reliance on the private sector and less reliance on government, trade liberalisation and the opening up of capital markets;

(2) The IMF would maintain its advisory and surveillance roles with respect to the policy reform programmes undertaken by the debtor countries. It would also collaborate with the World Bank in designing such adjustment programmes. The World Bank and the Regional Development Banks would provide increased lending over three years at the rates of $6 billion p.a. and $3 billion p.a., respectively, to support those debtor countries pursuing approved policy reform programmes; and

(3) The commercial banks would also increase their lending levels to $20 billion over three years. Such loans would be contingent on the debtor country's adoption of IMF-approved policy reforms as well as on its receipt of finance from the multilateral institutions.

The second part of the Baker Initiative, Baker II, was aimed at sub-Saharan Africa. This was called the Trust Fund Proposal because it was based on an IMF Trust Fund which was the outcome of principal repayments by these countries on former interest-free loans from the IMF. This would generate a flow of $2.7 billion special drawing rights or $3 billion for the purpose of implementing IMF/World Bank economic reform policies in the low income (i.e. annual p.c. incomes below $550) countries of sub-Saharan Africa.

Where does the Baker Plan fit in the typological framework developed above? It alters the nature of claims in the sense that it was designed to facilitate repayment flexibility without reducing the value of claims to creditors. The lack of success of the Baker Plan is by now widely accepted. What happened? Increased lending by the multilateral banks was slow to emerge. Although the commercial banks declared their support for the initiative, they did not follow through by increasing their lending. While many debtor countries made great progress in implementing programmes of economic reform, the sub-Saharan countries in particular found the IMF conditions to be too severe. The failure of the Baker Plan has been attributed to inadequacy of additional financing, the imposition by the IMF of politically unsustainable economic reform programmes on the debtor countries, a lack of appreciation of the realities of commercial banking, lack of specification of a role for creditor country governments and rejection of the principle of debt forgiveness. Indeed the emergence of the Brady Plan bears testimony to the official recognition of the failure of the Baker Plan.

By 1988, the Baker Plan was widely seen as incapable of providing any meaningful solution to the debt crisis. Commercial banks had taken steps to cover themselves against the risks associated with developing country debt. However, the servicing of huge debts continued to act as a brake on recovery in the debtor countries. The Japanese attempted to break the policy void at the Toronto summit of the Group of Seven Industrialised Countries. They offered funds that could be used to guarantee official agency debt relief. This did not lead immediately to a new initiative, however. It seems that the industrialised countries preferred to await the formation of a new US administration.

Low-income countries

President Mitterrand of France also made a proposal at the 1988 Toronto Summit which was designed to tackle the debt problems of low-income countries. It had been recognised for some time that the problems of severly indebted low-income countries (SILICs) – principally in Sub-Saharan Africa – differed from those of the severly indebted middle-income countries. For one it was considered that these countries suffered from more severe structural weakness and second the vast bulk of their debt is owed to multlateral agencies or is guaranteed by creditor country governments.[20] Feldstein et al. (1987) declared their debt problem one of insolvency rather than illiquidity.

A number of initiatives have been put in place for the low income countries. In December 1987 a three year (1988-90) World Bank Special Program of Assistance (SPA) was put in place for debt distressed low-income African countries.[21] The object of the programme is to increase concessional assistance, provide for quick disbursing and encourage debt relief. It is recognised that the short-term cash benefit of this programme will be small and that this type of programme will need to be enhanced.[22]

Arising from the 1988 Toronto summit of the G7 countries an agreement was reached to reschedule non-concessional bilateral official debt of low-income African countries at concessional rates. These reschedulings were to take place under the auspicies of the Paris Club. In addition what have come to be called the "Toronto Terms" are available only to countries that follow IMF or World Bank supported adjustment policies. Under Toronto Terms concessional debt is to be repaid with a twenty-five year maturity including a fourteen year grace period. Interest charges are to be at least as low as for the original loans. In fact many OECD countries have cancelled concessional debt. The terms for non-concessional loans are to be chosen from an option menu which includes stretching of maturities and grace periods.

More recently funds were made available in a scheme adopted at the September 1989 Annual Meeting of the IMF-World Bank in Washington which would enable (mainly) low-income African countries to receive up to $10 million on a grant basis in order to repurchase private claims on their government.

The case for debt relief in debt distressed low-income countries is overwhelming. Progress is being made in securing relief. However, the World Bank calculates that cash flow relief to date has not been substantial. The World Bank concludes that "[d]onor support beyond the horizon of current special programmes will be required. For SILICs outside of Africa no debt relief is in sight, and official action is urgently required".[23]

The most recent figures on the Toronto Terms confirm that they suffer from severe limitations: excluding Egypt, which benefited from exceptional debt reduction arising from its participation in the Gulf War, only $7 billion of the total African debt of $280 billion has so far been written off. The consequent interest payment reduction is around $200 million a year, compared to the $32 billion due each year and the $12 billion actually paid. Even full implementation of the Toronto Terms would reduce Africa's interest payments by no more than 5%.

Disappointment with the Toronto Terms has led some creditors to adopt the more generous Trinidad Terms, involving somewhat higher levels of debt relief though retaining the same conditionalities regarding eligibility for benefit. Unfortunately, some key creditors, most notably the US, have so far failed to endorse these terms. Also, it must be borne in mind that even full implementation of the Trinidad Terms would not necessarily go very far – $3-4 billion might be knocked off annual interest repayments due for Africa, but the impact on actual payments could be minimal (though, of course, any reduction in the debt overhang would be welcome).

The Brady Plan

For the middle-income countries the intent of the Bush administration as revealed in the initiative launched by the Treasury Secretary, Nicholas Brady in March 1989 has been the most significant official development. The major departure from the Baker Plan was the acceptance that debt forgiveness was a necessary element of any effort to solve the developing country debt problem. This Chapter will conclude with a brief discussion of the Brady initiative.

The nature of debt in Latin America and, in particular, the political stability of these debtors was a major strategic concern for George Bush when he took office in January 1989. New presidents had taken office in Mexico and Venezuela and each showed themselves willing to cooperate with IMF prescriptions for their countries. Within twelve months, elections were due in Argentina, Brazil, Chile, Colombia and Peru. It was clear that the reactions to the requests of Mexico and Venezuela for an easing of their debt burdens could influence the political outturns in these other countries. Therefore, from the strategic perspective of the US, there was an urgent need to offer some real hope of debt relief to these countries.

This offer came in the form of an initiative launched by US Treasury Secretary, Nicholas Brady, in March 1989. Brady suggested that the IMF and the World Bank should offer financial guarantees to encourage heavily indebted countries and their creditor banks to negotiate cuts in debt principal or interest. While the plan was sparse on details, it is significant in that it gives legitimacy to debt forgiveness. The basic idea was that creditor banks should accept "exit bonds" (whose value would be a mark down on the book value of debt) issued by debtors. Interest (maybe also at a concessional rate) would be guaranteed by the IMF and World Bank. The Japanese offer of finance at Toronto was to be used in building up a fund at the agencies to back these guarantees. Some commentators have suggested that the plan was an attempt "to combine America's cashless leadership with Japan's leaderless cash".[24]

There was also some suggestion that US domestic banking

policy might be altered in order to make it easier for US banks to tolerate reductions in the book value of the debt. This might include increasing the tax deductions that banks could claim for losses on Latin American loans and reducing the reserve requirements to cover these loans.

Brady did not make any specific proposals regarding the timing or mechanics for debt plans following his prescription. Indeed, the US Treasury confirmed that this was deliberate in that they did not wish to be seen to impose the details of plans. Their intention was that the fine points of any deal should be developed in negotiation between debtors and creditors.

The Brady proposal came under scrutiny at the Spring meetings of the IMF/World Bank in Washington in April. The debate revealed division among the G7 countries over the strategy. The US line was supported by France and Japan while the UK and West Germany formed the opposition. The joint communique issued suggested success for the US faction. It departed from earlier communiques in that it did not contain a warning that there should be no transfer of risk – arising from debt reduction – from the private sector to taxpayers of the industrialised countries. It was generally agreed, however, that the first real test of the Brady initiative would be the outcome of the Mexican debt renegotiation. Brady hoped that this would be completed in time for the July meeting of the G7 in Paris. This did not materialise and in the event, the deal was not concluded until 24 July 1989.

The Mexican deal presented a number of options to creditor banks:

"(1) To swap Mexican debt for new long-term bonds; Mexico to buy US Treasury securities to guarantee the principal.

(2) To switch from floating-rate debt, paying about 10% when the deal was announced, to new fixed rate debt paying 6.25%, without any change in face value; the interest rate to rise after 1996 if higher oil prices raise Mexico's oil revenues in real terms.

(3) To retain present claims but make new loans to Mexico over the next four years by enough to raise those claims by 25%; they will thus capitalise some of Mexico's debt-service payments".[25]

By October 1989 Costa Rica and the Philippines announced that they had also reached agreement in principle with their banks. The Brady initiative has come in for considerable criticism. Creditor banks, meeting in Washington during the IMF/World Bank Annual Meeting in September 1989 publically criticised the plan. The source of their discontent seems to be the nature of official guarantees and the fact that debt reduction has been officially sanctioned. They want more cash to be put up by multilateral agencies.

From the debtors' perspective, the extent of relief seems to be limited. Kenen (1990) argues that the reduction in the face value of Mexico's debt as a result of the July 1989 deal will be no larger than 16%. This is far short of the 35% reduction that many seemed to believe could occur. This is due to the fact all banks will not opt for the first option under the deal. *The Banker* magazine (October 1989) reports a similar assessment by the US credit rating agency Moody's. In a special report on the Brady initiative the agency argued that the plan would provide only very limited debt relief, while at the same time putting a new burden on the US banks which some of the weaker ones could find it difficult to bear.

The Brady initiative has made a positive contribution by placing debt reduction on the agenda – we argue the actual case for debt reduction in Chapter 7. However, the mechanism of debt relief is still in its formative stages. Bankers are unhappy because of official support for debt reduction. Debtors cannot expect much action in granting such relief until Brady is followed up with a more coherent proposal.

In practice, agreements under the Brady Plan have proven difficult and tedious to negotiate – only four were put in place during the two years after introduction of the Plan. In the case of Mexico there now appears to be relatively firm evidence of improved economic performance, arising, for example, from the knock-on effect of reduced domestic interest rates. The outcome in other countries is less clear-cut – for example, in the case of Costa Rica, the country suffered through the agreement's boosting of creditor confidence, which led to an increase in the secondary market price of debt.

Footnotes

1 Dornbusch, 1987, p. 40

2 Cline, 1984, p. 79

3 Ibid., pp. 30, 31

4 Ibid., p. 30

5 Ibid., p. 81

6 This is similar to the option that now exists in Ireland whereby house mortages can be taken out in say Deutsche Marks. The borrower pays German interest rates – currently lower – on this loan. She is exposed to exchange rate risk, however. If the Irish Punt, the currency in which she earns her income, is devauled against the Deutsche Mark, the currency in which she must repay her loan, her Irish Punt repayments will increase.

7 Chairman of the Municipal Assistance Corporation of New York and a partner in the investment banking firm of Lazard Freres & Co.

8 Cline op. cit., p. 85

9 Gutentag and Herring, 1983, p. 23

10 World Bank, 1987, p. 35

11 Cline, op. cit., p. 138

12 This can also be generalised to other types of options such as debt-for-nature swaps.

13 See Morgan Guaranty, *World Financial Markets*, September 1986, for evidence of this.

14 Blackwell and Nocera, 1988, p. 17

15 World Bank, 1989, p. 18

16 See Goureaux (1980) for an explanation of the CFF.

17 Defeasment is defined as the replacement of one bond issue by another.

18 This level of sales was disappointing. For an analysis, see Williamson, 1988, Appendix.

19 Williamson, 1988, p. 31

20 World Bank, 1989, p. 31

21 Some elements of the programme are available for countries outside of Africa, see World Bank, 1989 for details.

22 World Bank, 1989

23 Ibid., p. 33

24 *Business Week*, 8 May 1989

25 *The Economist*, 29 July 1989

Chapter 5

A Sample of Opinion

Introduction

Most participants will agree that solutions to the debt problem ought to be fair. This is hardly surprising since creditor and debtor alike would wish to be treated fairly. The participants will no doubt have a good idea of what they mean by fairness – a process or outcome that appears just to them. Commentators may also agree that solutions ought to be fair. However, it is difficult to operationalise this criterion so that it can be used in analysis of the situation. This problem is due to the difficulty of agreeing on what we mean by fairness in social interaction. In Chapter 6 we will formally develop the notion of fairness that is used in this study. This Chapter acts as a background for this discussion and a companion to the outline of plans and initiatives in the previous Chapter.

The impetus for this study was the view promulgated in the late 1980s that a solution to the debt crisis ought to be fair or just to debtor countries. This Chapter traces the development of this view. As we saw in the last Chapter debt reduction has now come to be officially endorsed by creditor countries. This can be interpreted as a move towards a solution which is fair to debtors. However, principles of fairness are not yet built into debt reduction schemes.

A major impetus to consider fairness as a criterion in devising solutions to the debt crisis was the 1987 call by the Pontifical Commission for an ethical approach to the debt problem. Whether it was an equal impetus to action is questionable. In the years since the publication of the Pontifical Commission Report, arguments for justice in the resolution of the debt crisis have emanated from a number of sources. These opinions were mainly directed against the orthodox approach to managing Third World debt whose purpose, it was argued, was concern for the stability of the world financial system and hence protection of the interests of the creditors.

This Chapter will proceed as follows. In the next section we will discuss aspects of the Catholic Church's views as they arise in the work of the Pontifical Commission and more recently the US bishops. The third section considers the evolving stance of the IMF and World Bank. Arguments made by NGOs and other popular interest groups are presented in the fourth section. This is followed by a review of the viewpoint put forward by UNICEF. A number of summary points are contained in the concluding section.

The Catholic Church

In January 1987, the Pontifical Commission on Justice and Peace issued a document entitled *At the Service of the Human Community: An Ethical Approach to the International Debt Question*. This document argued for the importance of considering the social and human dimensions of the debt problem in addition to purely economic and financial matters. Their starting point was the belief that "[d]ebt servicing cannot be met at the price of the asphyxiation of a country's economy, and no government can morally demand of its people privations incompatible with human dignity".[1] The terms of reference for the Commission, as set by the Pope, requested that they identify criteria for weighing the claims of all parties to the crisis in a just way and that they devise a method of analysis for "an ethical approach to the international debt question".

The Commission formulated six ethical principles. These are: solidarity – equal dignity for all nations and people; corresponsibility – sharing of responsibility for the causes of the debt problem; relations based on trust; effort and sacrifice sharing – sharing of the costs of adjustment on the basis of ability to pay; participation of all – broaden the set of active players; and ethics of survival – avoid outcomes that threaten the survival of players. These principles were then used to analyse the operation of an ethical solution to the debt problem. This analysis took the form of identifying the responsibilities of the various participants (players) in the debt problem.

Using the principle of ability to pay, the Commission argued that "the industrialised countries bear a heavier responsibility [than the debtors] which they must acknowledge and accept even if the economic crisis has often challenged them with grave problems of reconversion and employment".[2] They then go on to argue, on the basis of the solidarity principle, that industrialised countries have an obligation to: promote world growth but at the same time modify existing rules of international trade "which represent an obstacle to a more just distribution of the fruits of that growth"; unilaterally do away with protectionist measures which hinder exports from the developing countries; coordinate fiscal and monetary policies so as to reduce interest rates and exchange rate fluctuations; and bolster the price of raw materials.

In the Commission's opinion, coresponsibility requires that the debtor countries take an unjaundiced look behind the domestic causes of the increase in their overall indebtedness. Given the diversity among countries in this regard, a case by case approach is advocated as being more likely to provide "a more equitable evaluation of the coresponsibilities and the solutions adopted".[3]

Solidarity is offered as the principle that ought to guide developing countries. This principle has implications at three levels. Solidarity among the current and future citizens of a country requires that the leaders seek to promote sustained economic growth. International solidarity demands orderly trade between nations. The obligation on developing countries is to avoid excessive nationalism and be open to international links. Finally, regional solidarity calls for cooperation among debtors especially on economic matters.

In regard to the responsibilities of creditors with respect to debtors, the Commission is quite forthright. While the need for trust requires that the valid contracts of all parties be respected, it is argued that "creditors cannot demand contract fulfilment by any and all means, especially if the debtor is in a situation of extreme need".[4] It is recognised that commercial banks have obligations towards their depositors. However, the Commission believes that these banks also have a duty to debtors and that this latter obligation is more pressing. As a consequence actions that are directed towards fulfilling other obligations must be compatible with their duty to debtors. This is especially the case in what the Commission calls emergency situations, that is, those cases in which the countries lack solvency.

The Commission believes that creditors and debtors must jointly agree on plans to alleviate the debt problem. The creditor states, however, are responsible for finding repayment conditions that are "compatible with each debtor state's ability to meet its basic needs".[5]

The responsibilities of multilateral financial organisations, it is argued, are sevenfold: re-examination of IMF conditionality; promotion of dialogue towards debt rescheduling;

encouragement of new capital; macroeconomic coordination between industrialised countries; provision for altering terms in special circumstances (e.g. in the event of a natural disaster); research; and improved vetting and training of staff.

Of all the material we reviewed on the debt problem, and in particular the argument for justice in debt alleviation, we found the 27 September 1989 "Statement on Relieving Third World Debt" by the US Catholic Conference Administrative Board (1989) to be the most balanced and coherent in terms of analysis.

The statement argues that attention has focused on the situation of the creditors and the future of the international financial system. It suggests that few of the proposed remedies address the basic concern of social justice which the conference identifies as the question: "Why should the poor in debtor countries, who had nothing to say about accruing the debt and have received little or no benefit from it, have to pay the greater burden of its payment?" They note an actual increase of the debt burden and report that all those with whom they spoke, including bankers, led them to believe that there is a growing recognition among creditors of the need for debt reduction.

They then set out to apply principles of Catholic moral teaching to the debt problem. First they identify ethical arguments against the legitimacy of the debt in the aggregate. However, they note immediately that: "One does not, however, need to accept the argument that the debt is illegitimate to urge that there be relief from payment or even forgiveness in whole or in part, in order to lessen the sufferings of those most vulnerable to the effects of the debt burden".

This observation is, we believe, crucial. In Chapter 6 we will make an argument for the adoption of an "outcome" view of justice. As we will see the basis for justice in this context is not contained in a correcting of past wrongs. We actually argue against a concept of justice that would employ such a basis. The strength of the Conference's argument occurs when they argue on the basis of their observation noted above rather than on the basis of the moral illegitimacy of debt. In this their approach is very close to our own. The weakness in the Conference's statement is that it uses both types of argument.

The statement concludes with a number of recommendations. Among the recommendations are: total debt forgiveness is not appropriate for all states; a solution ought to preserve basic human rights and the independence of debtor countries; less money ought to leave debtor countries than enters; criteria for determining the amount of debt to be adjusted should include economic conditionality and considerations of human rights.

The IMF and World Bank

Following the Bretton Woods Agreement, 1944, the IMF was given the role of a monetary institution, with the authority to use contributed resources to provide short-term (less than 3 years) balance of payments (BOP) financing (loans) to member countries in deficit, on condition that these countries adopt policies, which the IMF considered appropriate, to deal with the problem. The latter has developed into what has become known as "IMF conditionality". The World Bank was given the role of a developmental institution, with the task of developing productive facilities in the developing countries and promoting the balanced growth of international trade. This role was translated into making loans available on favourable terms for approved development projects in developing countries.

The distinction between the two institutions in terms of their respective BOP and development financing functions has been all but wiped out by developments in the 1970s and 1980s. These developments include the IMF's willingness to finance relatively long-term (over three years) adjustment programmes and the World Bank's move, in 1980, into structural adjustment lending (i.e. loans to support major changes in policies and institutions in developing countries to help them overcome their current account deficits). Today the same set of policies and programmes tend to be financed jointly by the IMF and the World Bank.

We can distinguish four phases in the evolution of IMF/World Bank policy. These phases are broadly distinguished by a change in IMF/World Bank policy objectives and/or policy instruments. They are: (i) Pre-1982; (ii) 1982-86; (iii) 1986-88; and (iv) 1989-.

Pre-1982: In the early years of the IMF the typical IMF package consisted of policies with the aim of reducing aggregate demand in the short-run, for example: a reduction in state spending; some means of reducing wages, such as incomes/wage controls; a currency devaluation and possibly a reduction in trade controls. The hallmarks of a successful programme were considered to be an improvement in the current account of the BOP, a reduced fiscal deficit, lower inflation and more liberalised trade. This policy-approach prevailed with little modification until 1982.[6]

1982-86: In 1980, the IMF recognised that "payments imbalances prevailing in the international economy were structural in nature and therefore not amenable to correction over a short period of time."[7] The IMF admitted that the main problem in deficit countries was to create investment opportunities which would generate the productive resources required to close the gap between domestic production and consumption and recognised a need for policies to allow for higher levels of expenditure as well as higher growth rates over the medium term. Apart from the switch in emphasis from expenditure reduction to expenditure switching policies (as discussed in Chapter 3), the standard IMF package changed very little. After 1982, however, the IMF perception of an "acceptable" programme performance seems to have changed. Between 1982 and 1986, the emphasis was on improvements in the current account of the BOP with a greater toleration of inflation and persistent fiscal deficits. This might be seen as a pragmatic response conditioned by the emergency conditions which prevailed in this period.

1986-88: The next major change in policy coincides with the Baker Plan's focus on "adjustment with growth". Achievement of the latter, according to the IMF, required a combination of rapid trade liberalisation, devaluation, privatisation and financial reform. While this represented a continuation of the traditional IMF/World Bank "outward-orientation export promotion" growth policy, considerable emphasis was now put on movement towards free trade.

In April 1987, the World Bank staff produced a paper entitled "Protecting the Poor During Periods of Adjustment" for consideration by the Development Committee. This paper is important in that it sets out Bank thinking on the nature of adjustment it considers appropriate to deal with the economic crisis of developing countries. As the Bank sees it, countries do not have any choice but to adjust to the realities of the international economy. Their choice is between an "orderly adjustment programme and a haphazard one". They believe that adherence to the former will result in lower "social costs". In particular they argue that there is far less conflict than is generally supposed between "an adjustment programme's goals of efficiency and its effects on the poor".[8] Therefore, an adjustment programme should attempt to maximise the possibilities for growth subject to avoiding any unnecessary "transitional costs" for the poor. To this end, the Bank suggests that there are three important elements in an orderly adjustment programme: a growth orientation; credibility; and the necessity to secure additional external funding. The Bank does, however, recognise that there are two groups of countries – the highly indebted, middle income countries and the low income African countries in which the nature of the problems are quite different. The paper identifies two areas in which it believes that the Bank can play a role in protecting the poor during a period of adjustment. These are: aiding the rationalisation of public expenditure and investment with the object of redirecting social expenditures; and assisting efforts to compensate the poor directly through, for example, targeted nutrition and supplementary feeding programmes.

1989-: This period coincides with the Brady Plan and the official support for debt and debt service reduction. The IMF/World Bank views this approach as a continuation of the "growth with adjustment" policy orientation begun with the Baker Plan. Although this phase does not represent a policy objective change on the part of the IMF/World Bank, it does represent a policy instrument change. It represents a recognition by the IMF/World Bank of the failure of the Baker Plan – a recognition that net resource flows to developing countries were insufficient (mainly due to a shortfall in commercial bank lending) to support adjustment programmes.[9]

The NGOs

The President of the World Bank invited a response from NGOs on the 1987 staff paper mentioned in the previous section. The NGOs of the NGO-World Bank Committee nominated a group of five to prepare this reaction.[10] The comments were written up by John Clark of Oxfam (20 February 1987). The NGOs dissented on the nature of the main goal of adjustment programmes. They suggested that equity considerations should be at least as important as economic efficiency and growth and that the Bank should pursue a policy geared towards "adjustment with a human face". On this it was argued that "distributional considerations, taking into account the short as well as the long-term needs of the poor should be of paramount importance in framing adjustment programmes".[11] They went on to suggest that the Bank ought to officially acknowledge as legitimate the principle that it was acceptable that the pursuit of equity would involve costs in terms of slower economic growth and stabilisation.

The Liberian NGO, Susukuu, presented a response to the World Bank paper at a UN-NGO conference in September 1987.

It argued that the Bank failed to take account of the fact that those charged with implementing adjustment programmes – including the governments of developing countries – acted in their own self-interest and that this was often opposite to the interests of poorer groups in developing countries. When viewed from this perspective, Susukuu argued that adjustment programmes represented a damaging blow to the poor as they legitimised undemocratic regimes. They go further and claim that the supply of public funds is linked closely to the interests of western industrialised countries. The experience in countries such as Chile, Liberia, South Africa and Sudan suggests, they believe, that "the supply of public financial resources is inelastic with respect to efficiency and human rights considerations".[12]

An NGO conference on external debt, development and international cooperation was held in Lima during January 1988. The slogan of the conference was "Don't Pay the Unpayable". This conference attracted representatives of 41 NGOs from the North and 86 from the South. In its introduction to the conference proceedings the organising committee suggests that there are three campaign fronts on which NGOs should be operating: "challenging the legitimacy of the debt in law, mobilising opinion in favour of a cancellation of the debt, and support for the creation of an 'Indebted Countries Union' by the people's organisations".[13] The conference was quite diverse. In addition to addresses from government and NGO representatives, it included a set of groups working on topics prepared in a background paper and there were also a number of keynote speeches.

In his keynote address to the conference, Keith Griffin of Oxford University argued that debt default would be in the joint interest of debtors and the industrial sectors of developed countries. He discounted Baker-type solutions that would involve encouraging or forcing commercial banks to lend more to Third World countries and posited the opinion that "either some of the debt will have to be written off voluntarily by the creditor banks and countries or the debtor countries, explicitly or implicitly, will have to default". For the debtor countries, he suggested that there are three types of strategy: form a debtors' cartel; or agree on a policy of "default leadership"; or take unilateral default action. This one sided action is necessary, he suggests, because "government policy in the rich countries has supported the interests of international finance".[14] In doing this, he argues that they have neglected the interests of the debtor countries but also those of the industrial sectors of developed countries.

Griffin makes the point that the interests of debtors and creditor banks are diametrically opposed: the banks want their money back and wish to reduce their exposure to developing countries while the debtors want to reduce their debt service payments and make more resources available for growth. In the language of game theory their interaction is best characterised as a constant (in this case zero) sum game. On the other hand, he considers that the interests of debtors and the industrial sector of developed countries are linked because the debtors are potential markets for industrial goods. By acting on this commonality of interest, he believes that debtors could win an advantage in their conflict with creditors. He suggests that NGOs could play a crucial role in this endeavour by mobilising public opinion behind the case of the debtors. Recourse to historical precedence is also instructive, he suggests, because the Latin American defaults of the 1930s resulted in an enormous increase in the volume of imports and thereby assisted the recovery of industrial output in the advanced economies.

One of the most significant aspects of the conference is the fact that it reflects an attempt to organise a coalition against the continued servicing of the debt. As argued in the background document (which was revised for publication in March 1988):

"The fight for justice in each country is a means of challenging the creditors, for it is they who are benefiting from and adding to the injustices. The fight to achieve a real reduction in payments and to unite the debtor countries cannot be disassociated from the efforts to improve national living standards through genuine social progress".15

The line of thinking surveyed in the above paragraphs was synthesised at a meeting of the Permanent People's Tribunal in West Berlin which coincided with the joint meetings of the IMF/World Bank in September 1988. The tribunal was convened at the behest of the American Association of Jurists and was asked to consider "violations by the International Monetary Fund and the World Bank of international law in the self-determination of peoples and to make proposals for change". In assessing the economic and social context of the debt crisis, the tribunal concluded that the debt crisis in fact represents a crisis of the global development model. Further it argues that the IMF by doing its best to extract debt service from debtors is effectively acting in the interests of private lending institutions. They go on to argue that the IMF and World Bank have failed as institutions for regulation and crisis management and that they are therefore "responsible for the dramatic deterioration of the living conditions of the peoples in many parts of the world".[16] Having considered the various submissions, the tribunal reached a four point verdict. The final point in the verdict was:

"Considering the political and economic conditions that generated it, the repudiation of debt can be justified by the 'defence of necessity' which is accepted by the international courts as a valid defence when payment of financial obligations would gravely impair the living standards of a nation's population – as is the case with all Third World countries".[17]

On this basis, they argued for a general moratorium on debt and the convening of an international negotiating conference. They suggested, however, that this conference should: write-off debt; transform external debt into local currencies to finance regional development funds; and transfer the advantages of the operation of secondary markets to the debtors. Creditors would be unlikely to consider a forum with such terms of reference a negotiating conference, however! In addition, they argue that adjustment policies must be fair – that is, a policy would be considered justifiable only if it satisfied the following criteria: political viability, social acceptability, and environmental responsibility.

UNICEF

The NGOs made a reference to "adjustment with a human face" in their comments on the World Bank paper. This in fact was the theme of a UNICEF study which grew out of their 1983 report *The Impact of World Recession on Children.* In 1987, UNICEF published volume 1 of this study which analysed the nature of adjustment in the developing world during the 1980s and proposed an alternative adjustment strategy. This was followed by a second volume of case studies which was published in 1988. Within its frame of reference this is a major contribution to "development thinking".[18] It is beyond the scope of our study to consider this report in detail. However, we must note its significance as an opinion forming document since it is far more comprehensive and considered than the papers mentioned above. It synthesises recent thinking on an ethical or equitable approach to development. As a result, it has the greatest potential to influence public opinion and action in the developed world.

UNICEF accepts that the deterioration of conditions in the developing world in the last decade necessitates adjustment. It dissents from the conventional approach to adjustment –

"by which reduction of external and internal imbalances is achieved by demand and import restraints, often entailing a decline in GDP as well as investment in physical and human capital" – and argues that "adjustment with a human face is a pre-condition for long-term growth". The study is concerned with identifying the justification, nature and possibilities for such a plan and defines adjustment with a human face as involving "a restructuring of the economy so that major imbalances are eliminated at a satisfactory level of output and investment while human capacities are maintained and developed".[19]

In order to achieve an orderly and equitable growth orientated adjustment, it is argued that: the trading environment must be improved so as to ensure a sustained expansion of Third World export earnings; and the capital account must be transformed by reversing the negative resource transfer.[20] The following changes would be needed to achieve such an end:

- improved macroeconomic coordination among industrial-ised countries directed towards promoting steady growth of the world economy;[21]
- a halt to threatened further protectionism and the dismantling of existing restrictions;
- the use of commodity price agreements to support the real earnings of poor countries from primary commodity exports;
- restoration of positive net resource flows to developing countries by increasing the inflow of public and private resources;
- reduction of real interest rates;
- debt restructuring and/or debt relief.

The ethical principle underlying these arguments is that policy should be directed towards improving the well-being of the worst-off group in developing countries – the children. In the first chapter of volume one, Cornia assesses the pattern of economic decline and human welfare in the first half of this decade. He finds that there was "a widespread and sharp reversal in the trend toward the improvement in standards of child health, nutrition, and education".[22] Adopting the expectation that the economic problems of the early part of this decade will persist, he suggests that the declining trend in the welfare of children will continue "unless radical measures are taken in the area of debt and capital flows and unless a strong recovery in the industrial market economies revitalises world trade, and with it commodity prices".[23] On the basis of such arguments, the UNICEF study calls for the reorientation of development policy as a "basic needs" approach to adjustment. They see this as the fourth phase of post-war development policy – the first three being; the growth maximisation stage of the 1950s and 1960s; the 1970s phase where basic needs/poverty alleviation became the focus of development; and the concentration on adjustment without regard to distribution during the early 1980s.

Conclusion

Debt forgiveness of some form is now firmly on the agenda. This may eventually give rise to criteria of equity/fairness being applied in debt negotiations. Indeed, when US Treasury secretary Brady unveiled his March 1989 initiative he stated that "[o]ur policy is to rekindle the hope of the people and leaders of debtor nations that their sacrifices will lead to greater prosperity in the present and the prospect of a future unclouded by the burden of debt".[24]

Debt forgiveness embraces many possible outcomes. An acceptance by the economic powers of a need for forgiveness may not result in policies that those in favour of an ethical solution would consider as meeting this objective. It is therefore necessary that the meaning of ethics or equity be clear and that there be some sort of agreed measure for assessing policies against this criterion. We believe that this has not been adequately done to date and it is the objective of this study to go some way towards correcting this deficiency. This exercise is useful for two groups of readers – NGOs and similar organisations who are interested in making the ethical case and the general reader who wishes to assess whether the ethical case is persuasive.

In the next part of this study we attempt to demonstrate how economics principles can be used in making the ethical/equity case.

Footnotes

1 Pontifical Commission Report, 1987, p. 4
2 Ibid., p. 17
3 Ibid., p. 20
4 Ibid., p. 25
5 Ibid.
6 Some modifications include: the issue of special drawing rights (SDRs), a form of unconditional international credit which may be used to cover BOP deficits;

the compensatory financing facility (CFF), a fund created in 1963 to deal with short-term shortfalls in export earnings; and the "Oil Facility" in 1974-75, a fund with low conditionality to deal with deficits resulting from the 1973-74 oil crisis.

7 See M. Guitan "Economic Management and IMF Conditionality", in Killick (ed.) *Adjustment and Financing in the Developing World*, Washington: IMF, 1982, p. 86.

8 Having reviewed the evidence on the deterioration of social conditions in developing countries, the authors make the following statement. "Almost none of the studies producing this evidence, however, tried to determine whether the social deterioration was the outcome of adjustment policies, the legacy of past policies, or the unfavourable international economic environment. Indeed, most of the examples pre-date the initiation of adjustment policies. Nonetheless, there has been a tendency to associate much of the deterioration with adjustment programmes – and to blame the deterioration on neglect of the "social costs of adjustment" (World Bank, 1987, p. 3).

9 For additional historical details, see Guitan (1982) and Killick (1982)

10 In fact they were asked to comment on a pre-April 1987 draft of the paper.

11 Clark, 1987, p. 1

12 Susukuu, 1978, p. 4

13 Lima Conference, 1988, p. 10

14 Griffin, 1988, pp. 89-90

15 Lima Conference, 1988, pp. 62, 63

16 Permanent People's Tribunal, 1988, p. 14

17 Ibid., p. 22

18 UNICEF sought to produce a study which would be directed at those directly involved in the making of adjustment policy. In doing this it adopted an economic frame of analysis and made proposals that could be operationalised within the existing economic order.

19 Cornia, Jolly, Stewart, 1987, p. 294

20 Helleiner and Stewart, 1987, p. 277

21 To many this may come across as somewhat of a truism. However, it should be noted that while economists may favour the expansion of the world economy, they may not accept that explicit coordination between countries is required to promote it. In this regard it is interesting to consider the reply given by Laurence Summers (an economic adviser to Michael Dukakis during his 1988 bid for the US presidency) in a Challenge (June/July 1988) interview to a question seeking to ascertain whether there were any differences between him and Martin Feldstein. (Summers was a student and is now a close colleague of Feldstein's. Feldstein was a Chairman of the Council of Economic Advisers under Ronald Reagan and has also acted in an advisory role to George Bush.) Summers replied that he supported international macroeconomic coordination while Feldstein did not.

22 Cornia, 1987, p. 34

23 Ibid., p. 20

24 *The Irish Times*, 11 March 1989, p. 6

Chapter 6 ▉▉▉▉▉▉▉▉▉▉▉

The Idea of Fairness

Introduction

The present Chapter is concerned with specifying an idea of fairness that can be used in evaluating suggested plans for the alleviation of the debt crisis. In particular we will examine the meaning of the terms ethics, equity, fairness, and justice and consider the ways in which economists have attempted to operationalise them.

The idea of fairness in social interaction is at once conceptually difficult and profoundly important. For those who believe that fairness should be centre stage in any discussion of Third World debt and development, these facts present a challenge. In order to convince others of the importance of fairness arguments, it is necessary to have formulated and be able to communicate your notion of fairness. If you are not able to do this, the persuasive power of your argument will be diminished. The current Chapter explains the formulation of our notion of fairness.

This task requires us to outline some important arguments that occur in the branch of economics known as theoretical welfare economics. We are conscious that this is apt to make reading of the Chapter demanding. Readers may wonder whether discussion of such issues is necessary. In our opinion it is. This is especially so on account of the weight that is often attached to the evidence of expert witness. Proposed solutions to the debt crisis are often advocated or dismissed on the basis of their "efficiency properties". Efficiency is a theoretical concept used in economics. As with many scientific economics concepts, the word efficiency also has interpretations in ordinary language. It is important to be aware of what the scientific meaning of efficiency does and does not imply.

There is a popular impression that efficiency is some sort of absolute, value-free, concept. For this reason an argument based on efficiency considerations is often seen as conclusive. In arguing against the conclusion of such an argument, you are then implicitly seen as being against "what is best". In fact, the concept of efficiency as used by economists is *not* value-free. Furthermore, there are many possible efficient outcomes depending on the initial distribution of resources. A consequence of this is that the concept of efficiency cannot be used to justify a particular property distribution. This point is often overlooked. Efficiency in terms of how resources are allocated is a very powerful concept, but it is important to recognise what it does and does not imply.[1]

Economics principles

In discussing the fairness of proposed solutions to the external debt problem of Third World countries, commentators use a number of terms. These terms are often used interchangeably. However, there are subtle differences between the terms. Misunderstanding can be avoided by formally defining these terms. We will begin with this exercise.

Consider the following terms: "fair", "equitable", "ethical", and "just". They can be defined as follows: "fair" – in accordance with the rules; "equitable" – fair/impartial; "just" – giving proper consideration to the claims of everyone concerned; "ethical" – morally correct. Each term is similar in that each refers to the process or outcome being in accordance with the rules of the game. This in turn raises other questions: What are the rules of the game? How are these rules formlated? On what principles are these rules based? One principle that seems common to the terms is that all parties to a transaction be treated in the same way. This in turn may require the equalisation of opportunities. In this way outcomes will differ only to the extent that people's talent and effort differs.

The dictionary definitions suggest a qualitative difference between the last term and the other three in that it refers to morality. Therefore, in saying that something is ethical we might mean that it conforms to people's sense of what is right and not just legal rights or obligations. In this study ethics will be the principles underlying the rules of the game. The terms equity, justice and fairness will be used to evaluate a state of the world in relation to this ethical code.[2]

The purpose of this section is to demonstrate how it is necessary to explicitly build in ethical principles when answering certain types of questions from an economic point of view. We will see how this requirement causes difficulty in identifying a common basis on which to conduct analysis. Most of all, however, we hope to demonstrate that: ethical principles underlie much of economic analysis and as a consequence one must be aware of these principles when interpreting the conclusions of such analysis. There is a widespread impression that economic analysis is value-free and that its perspective dominates others. It is not and it does not. Many commentators seek to use economics to buttress their ideological biases. It is better to expose this for what it is rather than to dismiss economics.

Economists have long been aware of the problems inherent in applying standards of fairness in policy matters. The classic distinction drawn in introductory textbooks is between questions that concern "what is" as opposed to "what ought to be". The former type of question, involving as it does the acceptance of the status quo, is straightforward. Questions of the latter type involve comparing the well-being of people. To the extent that a particular policy will involve one person gaining at the expense of another, the economist is confronted with a difficult problem. Once it is accepted that no quantitative basis exists for comparing the gains and the losses, one must resort to the enunciation of principles.

Our concern in this monograph is with the desirability of various plans for the alleviation of the debt burden on Third World countries. While we focus on the problems of the debtors, we cannot arbitrarily neglect the welfare of the other parties to the crisis. It is useful to begin with an analogy to the problem we are considering. Taxation is the major source of finance for funding government policy. The methods of applying taxation are numerous. They can be classified in a number of ways. One such classification would relate to who actually pays the tax. In other words, how is the burden of the tax to be shared? This is similar to the question which is of concern here: how is the burden of adjustment from the debt crisis to be shared among creditor and debtor?

Some will disagree with this analogy. Their argument might take the following form. A government pursuing taxation policy is laying down the terms of a social contract. It is, therefore, valid to consider equity in drafting such a contract. On the other hand there already exists a contract between creditor and debtor which came into existence at the time of the initial transaction. Therefore, other parties have no right to compromise the creditors by suggesting a renegotiation of the contract now. There are two grounds on which we can question this argument. One relates to the position of the parties at the time of making and implementing the contract – this is the rights/process view. The other concerns future possibilities – the outcome perspective.

The rights/process view

If the initial contract and/or its implementation involved a violation of justice to the debtors, one might argue that the contract ought to be void. Many would take this view. The Permanent People's Tribunal, for instance, considered that the issue of "a duty of reparation on behalf of the victims of the bad management of the debt crisis" as an important topic that it had to consider.[3] Point three of its verdict finds that "The World Bank has been negligent in that it has made loans without properly examining the needs of the debtor nations, nor has it considered fully the ability of the debtor nations to repay such loans. The structural policy of the World Bank/IMF caused a growing net transfer of resources from indebted countries into the creditor countries. Consequently, lives and living standards in indebted countries have deteriorated. The environment has been irreversibly damaged and living areas of indigenous peoples have been destroyed. *The payment of reparations should therefore be considered.* Through such practices the IMF/World Bank gave illusory legitimacy to the accumulation strategies of the industrial countries, MNCs and international finance capital, which led to the present disaster. A disaster imperilling, not only the present but the future of most nations".[4]

This is a legal point of view which seeks to identify the likely cause for an event and suggest reparation. Is it a persuasive argument and will it lead to the suggested action? Opinion of this sort from formal or semi-formal international judicial bodies abound. They often identify wrongdoings by powerful nations against weaker ones. The opinions are often ignored by the aggressor nations – witness the reaction of the US to rulings against the illegality of its interventions in Nicaragua. This reaction clearly relates to relative power. However, we also believe that it is related to the weakness of this type of argument.

Third World Debt : Towards an Equitable Solution

There exists neither an implicit nor explicit world constitution that gives legitimacy to the rulings of such international judiciaries. Their power rests on international association and agreement. Therefore the philosophical basis of the type of argument is going to be important in determining its effectiveness.

Adams[5] has highlighted the legal notion of "odious debts" – debts contracted for illegitimate purposes by illegimate parties. She notes that a case for repudiation of a state's debt can be based on the argument that the debt of a predecessor government is "odious". Cases from the late nineteenth and early twentieth centuries are invoked, though there have been no cases recently. What chances of success would such a case now have? There are two elements to consider: *ultra vires* (legality of contracting authority) and the use of the debt. A case based on *ultra vires* is unlikely to be successful and the generality of purpose militates against success on the second count. This is simply our opinion regarding the likelihood of success. We have not yet commented on whether Adams advances an appropriate concept of equity. A philosophical assessment of the overall rights/process view is discussed below.

There is a long philosophical tradition that interprets justice in a rights/process mode. This tradition includes Kant and Nozick. Robert Nozick, for instance, would argue that it is important to consider the justice of the historical process that leads to the current outcome. A lack of justice would give grounds to the injured party to seek a reshuffle of entitlements. Samuel Brittan[6] points out that this idea is also contained in the Old Testament. In Chapter 25 of Leviticus, reference is made to a jubilee every 50 years in which all land would return to its original owners, debt cancelled, slaves freed and the land left fallow. In other words violations of justice in transfer and acquisition committed by one's ancestors would be rectified. But as Brittan says, we need a theory of just acquisition of property rights in the first place in order to operationalise this concept.

The line of thinking that emerges from this approach to justice is often called the "desert" or "productivity" theory of fairness – an individual deserves to retain what she earns or produces. The basis of this viewpoint can either be a belief that individuals have "natural rights" with justice being violated when individuals are deprived of these rights or an emphasis on the need for "fair rules and processes" with the outcome being deemed fair if the process is fair.[7] The difficulty for this school of thought is in identifying absolute rights and the weight to be given to "fair process".

Many possible absolute rights have been cited such as the right to life, free speech and private property.[8] But are these rights absolute? Should free speech be tolerated to the extent that an individual can shout "fire" in a crowded cinema? US Justice Holmes did not think so. While the problem of identifying the set of absolute rights is severe the real problem is in deciding on what happens when one individual's supposed absolute rights conflict with those of another as with the example above where one individual's right to free speech conflicts with the right to free assembly of others.

On the question of the weight to be given to "fair process", Abelson has drawn a useful distinction between the strong and very strong viewpoint.[9] The former, which Abelson considers defensible, argues that outcomes can never be considered independently of the process that generates the outcome. Abelson offers the following illustration: "If two equally able individuals start the day equally wealthy and one works and the other does not, most people would consider it fairer for the worker to keep his product than that it be equally shared". This conclusion, however, could emerge from a consideration of incentive effects even if one did not adhere to the rights/process philosophy.[10] The very strong position, Abelson argues, would appear to hold that fair processes are both necessary and sufficient. The sufficiency of fair process as a condition of fairness is difficult to accept since initial conditions are neglected. As Boadway and Bruce[11] argue: "If one begins with a postulate, 'individuals have rights', as Nozick does, and if one defines these rights to include whatever social institutions one seeks to defend (e.g. the distribution of income as determined by the existing system of property rights) then there is little left to say except that one's conclusions follow (trivially) from one's premises (or is it vice versa?)". We are, therefore, led to the conclusion that the rights/process view requires a theory of the just acquisition of property rights and, as Brittan argues, neither Nozick or others have provided such a theory.[12]

We will, therefore, have difficulty in countering the validity of leaving the existing debt contracts in place on this basis. One side can argue for their policy on the basis of the property rights of creditors, while the other derive their conclusions from consideration of the rights to subsistence of the debtors. Each argument may be perfectly consistent with the rights that are being considered immutable. However, adherence to the rights/process view of justice offers no scope for resolution. It is for this reason that we believe one must look towards an alternative conception of justice.

The outcome view

The argument for making an analogy between the debt crisis and taxation can be strengthened by considering the purpose of tax reform. Remember that no government is laying down a social contract ab initio. There is already in place a set of rights and obligations. A major tax reform may alter the outcomes for different groups. If we follow the logic of the argument for keeping the contract no such reform should be contemplated. However, those who argue for honouring debt contracts to the letter are not averse to tax reform. If we trace the justification for tax reform we may find a basis for considering alterations of debt contracts.

The argument for tax reform is based on some notion of improving on the current outcome. Therefore, the possibility of improving the lot of society ultimately, allows one to transcend the rights inherent in present arrangements. In other words some rights are more basic than others. It is on this basis that we believe that it is valid to talk about altering present arrangements in debt contracts. An historical righting of wrongs is not a useful objective. The prospect of improving on the current outcome is a more compelling reason for altering present arrangements.

The basis for this view rests on an alternative conception of justice to that we reviewed above. We shall refer to it as the outcome view of justice, although it is also referred to as the social welfare or utilitarian philosophy. Abelson explains that outcome views of fairness in their crudest form are based on the assumption that the end justifies the means.[13] In other words, redistribution by coercion is justified if it produces a fairer society and if it does not destroy the incentive to create wealth. The guiding principle is the postulate of "asset egalitarianism", which has been defined by Arrow as the belief that all the assets of society, including personal skills, are available as a common pool for whatever distribution required by justice.[14] In particular, redistributive policies which take the product of some individuals and give it to others are just if they raise social welfare, appropriately defined. In regard to taxation, a typical implication of this approach is the principle of "ability to pay".[15] This is the conception of justice which underlies modern welfare economics.

In this study we follow the "outcome" approach. This is not to suggest that we can "prove" that this is the superior view. Each approach faces a fundamental difficulty in application. The process view requires a theory of the just acquisition of property rights while the outcome view needs some means of ranking end states. Our bias reflects the tradition of modern welfare economics which concentrates on this latter task. The next section outlines the criteria that we will follow.

Equity criteria

In using equity considerations in evaluating proposals for the alleviation of the debt crisis, we will need a means of operationalising the outcome view of justice. For this purpose we will use the following criteria: liberty; efficiency; vertical equity; horizontial equity. In order to explain why we use these terms, it is first necessary to consider some aspects of formal economic theory. This involves formally notions of efficiency and equity. Both of these involve normative considerations in that they are concerned with ranking states of society according to some social ordering of preferences. They differ in the extent of the value judgements involved.

Efficiency

Efficiency, as used by economists, makes use of two value judgements in ranking social states. The first, called individualism, asserts that the individual is the best judge of her own preferences – in other words, their preferences should not be dictated by some authority. The second is the so-called "Pareto Principle". In its strongest form, this says the following: if state of society A is ranked higher than B by one person, and all other persons rank A at least as high as B, then the social ordering should rank state A higher than B.

In popular debate, economic efficiency is often used as an argument for a particular policy. It is important to realise that this concept is not value free as is sometimes suggested. The use made of this concept to justify outcomes in the market economy is at times tenuous. However, the notion of efficiency does play an important role in welfare or normative economics. It is useful to explain the nature of this role.

The price system is a means of coordinating decisions in decentralised economies. It performs this role by communicating information to buyers and sellers. A strong case can be made for the value of the price system as a coordinator.[16] How good is the outcome of this process? The answer clearly depends on what is meant by good. Economists use efficiency as a measure of goodness. They then proceed to examine the efficiency of the price system. The fundamental theorems of welfare economics are the outcome of this exercise.

A brief description of these results serves to highlight the applicability and limitations of statements about efficiency. Remember, however, that these theorems relate to logical constructions which are not descriptions of the real world. Therefore, just because we know something is true in these constructions does not mean that it is true in the real world. More importantly, if we are unsure about something in these models then we certainly cannot claim to know much about the real world effect of this item.

The first fundamental theorem asserts that under certain conditions the outcome of the price/market system is efficient. This outcome will be the result of the interaction of buyers and sellers starting from an initial state. The theorem does not say that the initial state is efficient. To the extent that different outcomes will emerge depending on the starting point, the theorem is neutral on the starting point. The initial state refers to the claims to property such as the holdings of resources and claims on profits.

Must we accept property rights as given and so be content with the subsequent outcome of the market? The second theorem addresses this question. It is possible that there are a large number of efficient outcomes with a particular distribution of income associated with each one. The theorem states that any one of these efficient states can be achieved as the outcome of the price system via a distribution of initial property.

Therefore, the concept of efficiency can be used to argue the case of the market as a coordinator. It cannot be used to argue that the current outcome is the unique best. Application of the notion of efficiency involves identifying the conditions under which the market will achieve such an outcome. For instance, one such condition is that the benefits and costs perceived by individual decision makers are in accord with the benefits and costs to society in general. If they are not, as in the case of a polluter not bearing the consequences of his actions, the outcome of the market will not be Pareto optimal. Economists then proceed to identify policies, such as a pollution tax, to correct these market failures.

Policy interventions that seek to promote efficiency proceed by attempting to identify and correct impediments to the operation or "imperfections" of the market. The argument made by World Bank staff in their April 1987 paper "Protecting the Poor during Periods of Adjustment" is in this tradition since it sees considerable scope for adjustment programmes that improve efficiency and well-being. Does there exist such scope? For this to be established we would need to show where market imperfections would arise. The Bank's paper does not attempt to do this and instead proceeds on the presumption that the scope for improved efficiency exists. They justify this by reference to wasteful expenditures. This is not satisfactory. For a proper analysis, it is important to explain why the market does and does not work under different circumstances and to draft policy on this basis.

Social choice when individuals disagree

Efficiency is one focus on which to build debt alleviation proposals. It is appealing in that it involves some gaining while no one loses, i.e, it accords with the Pareto Principle discussed above. In many cases changing the distribution of income involves some gaining at the expense of others. In the context of the framework outlined above, the value judgements underlying efficiency are not sufficient in deciding whether to leave existing property rights intact or to initiate redistribution. There may be many efficient states.[17] The problem now is to identify the best of these states. But best here is defined with respect to some ethical principles that have not been stated. To proceed, we need to outline these value judgements.

Economists use a device known as the "social welfare function" to codify value judgements. It is the means by which the outcome view of justice is operationalised. Its basic feature is to define the various actions and institutions in terms of their contribution to the well-being of society as measured by some social welfare index. The form of the function[18] will differ depending on the set of value judgements. Which ethical principles ought to be built into this social ordering? This is the most difficult question that we will confront. Graff clarifies the nature of the problem and offers useful advice in this regard: "... can we somehow distil the various ethical beliefs of the members of a community into a consistent system, suitable for our purposes and capable of telling us how to 'add' one man's welfare to another's? The answer clearly depends on the extent to which we require *detailed* ethical judgements. If fairly broad ones will do, then we can reasonably hope to find sufficient consilience of opinion in a moderately homogenous society to enable us to proceed. But if agreement is required on matters of detail as well as on matters of principle, we are unlikely to be so lucky.

One of the things we must continually bear in mind, therefore, is the *specificity* of the ethical assumptions we find ourselves making. We want to keep them as broad as possible, so that interest in our conclusions may be widespread. But we also want them to be detailed enough to yield some conclusions".[19]

As we mentioned earlier, a basic tenet of welfare economics is that the social orderings of states respect individual rankings, i.e. the individual is considered to be the best judge of his/her own preferences. The design of the social welfare function is therefore concerned with the way in which we aggregate individual preferences. The original approach was to adopt the so-called "utilitarian ethic". This criterion defines the total happiness of society as the sum of well-being across every member. Society is better-off the larger this sum. This approach has been criticised because of the need to make interpersonal comparisons of well-being (for a given change we need to compare the change in the well-being of the loser with that of the gainer) and because the distribution of income that maximises total happiness may not itself be desirable. This raises the more fundamental question of how one is to *derive* the social welfare function.

The best known and perhaps most important attempt to lay out specifically the method of arriving at a social welfare function is the work of John Rawls (1971). The central part of Rawls's work, according to Arrow (1973), is a statement of fundamental propositions about the nature of a just society. He seeks to justify these propositions by arguing that they would be the ones that would emerge from a contract made among rational potential members of society. He then investigates the implications of these propositions for the design of social institutions. The general proposition that would emerge according to Rawls is asset egalitarianism (which we defined above). The more specific statements on the nature of justice that he derives consist of two parts. Arrow offers a succinct description of these. "First, among the goods distributed by the social order, *liberty* has a priority over others; no amount of material goods is considered to compensate for a loss of liberty. Second, among goods of a given priority class, inequalities should be permitted only if they increase the lot of the least well-off". The first statement is known as the priority of liberty and the second is generally known as the maximin principle although Rawls himself called it the "difference principle".[20]

This maximin rule would on the face of it lead to equalisation of income. However, it is recognised that this may not be in the interests of society because of adverse incentive effects. In other words, the application of maximin in its purest form would result in 100% taxation above a certain level with corresponding subsidies below this level. The incentive to exert effort by the more able could be diminished by this policy and this would in turn reduce the well-being of the less able. Therefore, a more graduated tax schedule would be appropriate. Attempts by economists to identify the exact graduation have proven problematic, however.

The need for graduation in taxation raises another problem. To the extent that a tax is levied on the basis of ability, individuals will not have an incentive to reveal their true preferences. Incentive considerations must therefore be taken into account in framing policy.

It is interesting to note that this Rawlsian approach seems popular with some of the commentators we surveyed in the Economics Principles section of this chapter. The Permanent People's Tribunal argues that its "jurisdiction has to be strongly supportive of the most vulnerable groups, not only the whole of the peoples of the indebted countries but more specifically the most disadvantaged social groups in those countries without omitting the growth of large areas of poverty and deprivation in the industrialised countries".[21] A similar sentiment is expressed in the NGO response to the World Bank (1987) paper: "we think it is a great mistake to group all of the poor together as one homogenous group...in particular special thought should be given to the *poorest*".[22]

Two competing views of justice therefore seem to be present in some arguments. The Tribunal's argument that the defence of necessity should be used in favour of the debtors is certainly outcome related.

Finally, there is a principle called "horizontal equity" that is often used in the economics literature. It is usually defined as saying that "equals should be treated equally". There is some debate as to how this should be interpreted. We prefer the interpretation associated with Musgrave that horizontal equity be seen as a "safeguard against capricious discrimination".[23] Interpreted in this light it is a concern with the means to achieve results rather than with the outcomes themselves. In other words, it is a concern that individuals not be treated differently on the basis of irrelevant characteristics. The value judgement arises in identifying which characteristics are "relevant".[24]

Summary

In summary, therefore, the outcome view of justice can be operationalised with the aid of four criteria. These can be applied to the evaluation of proposals to alleviate the debt crisis.

1. Liberty

The notion of liberty, Rawls argues, requires that: "each person engaged in an institution or affected by it has an equal right to the most extensive liberty compatible with a like liberty for all".[25] Liberty refers to, what Rawls calls, "opportunities of citizenship", such as freedom of conscience and basic civil rights. Rawls suggests that the most basic principle of justice is the "priority of liberty". According to this, the loss of freedom for some cannot be justified by an improvement in the economic well-being of others. Thus, while the outcome approach considers that the assets of society are available for redistribution so as to make the society more just in economic terms, this must proceed in a context that respects basic liberties.

The remaining criteria can be thought of as rules of thumb to be used in achieving economic justice.

2. Efficiency

Policy interventions that seek to promote efficiency proceed by attempting to identify and correct impediments to the operation, or "imperfections", of the market. The principle involves "weak" ethical criteria in that it can only be used in comparing states of society where some may be made better off without making anyone worse off. Some may see this as a very limited concept of efficiency and, indeed, in order to have a more complete ordering of social states, it is necessary to supplement this criterion.

3. Vertical equity

The ability to pay – the maximin principle in its operational mode – criterion accepts inequalities only if they increase the lot of the least well-off. On the face of it, this rule would lead to equalisation of income. However, it is recognised that this may not be in the interests of society because of adverse incentive effects. In other words, the incentive to exert effort by the more able could be diminished by this policy and this would in turn reduce the well-being of the less able. Therefore, a partial equalisation is usually favoured.

4. Horizontal equity

The principle of horizontal equity, we have said, is usually defined as saying that "equals should be treated equally". There is some debate as to how this should be interpreted. We prefer the interpretation associated with Musgrave that horizontal equity may be seen as a "safeguard against capricious discrimination". In other words, it is a concern that individuals not be treated differently on the basis of irrelevant characteristics.

Footnotes

1 It is interesting to observe such people quote Adam Smith's doctrine of the "invisible hand" as if Smith's metaphor proved a case. Smith identified a possibility. As Mark Blaug (1978) points out, Smith's argument on this point was quite weak. It was only in the 1950s work of such economists as Kenneth Arrow that "Smith's theorem" was fully analysed. On the issue of the interaction of economic theory and the political organization of society, Arrow's autobiographical essay (Dissent, 1978) is recommended to specialists and non-specialists alike. The cautious nature of the conclusions reached by one of this century's most outstanding economists is in sharp contrast to the great certainties that much less able commentators believe they can derive from economic theory.

2 It is interesting to see that left wing politicians have begun to integrate more rigorous thought about the market into their thinking. This is no doubt the result of an attempt to challenge the simplistic notions of the market professed by their right wing colleagues. It is encouraging to see this type of a reaction rather than the knee jerk rejection of the market that has been prevalent in the past. For an interesting example of the recent socialist view from an active politician the reader is referred to the Chapter "There Must be Markets" in Roy Hattersley's 1987 book *Choose Freedom*.

3 Permanent People's Tribunal, 1988, p. 16

4 Ibid., pp. 21, 22

5 Adams, 1991, p. 164

6 Brittan, 1988, p. 221

7 Abelson (1987) attributes the former emphasis to Kant, Nozick, and Peacock and Rowley and the latter to Buchanan and Weber.

8 The distinction between traditionalist and modernist thinking in Ireland identified by Barry (1988) can be related to this discussion. One could re-phrase his argument in terms of a distinction between a rights/process view of justice and an outcome view of justice. In this light the similarity in approach of "right to life" and "right to choose" arguments is understandable.

9 Abelson, 1987, p.4

10 Indeed it is such considerations that make the benefit principle of taxation acceptable to those who hold the outcome view of justice (Boadway and Bruce, 1984, p.176).

11 Broadway and Bruce, 1984, p. 177

12 Brittan, 1988, p. 221

13 Abelson, 1987, p. 5. This is a fairly bald statement that could alarm many people. As we will see below the outcome view does not suggest some form of totalitarianism. In the context of the statement made in the text, consider the following point. In order to make welfare payments to the poor, others will

need to have their income taxed. Some libertarians would consider this to be theft. They essentially make no difference between a situation where an individual actually robs them and a situation where an individual gets a welfare payment as a consequence of their being taxed. In the context of the outcome approach we suggest that this latter "organised" removal of income is justified because it makes society somehow a "better place".

14 Arrow, 1973, p. 248

15 Broadway and Bruce, 1984, p. 176

16 The classic argument is due to Hayek. Research in recent years, however, takes the view that all information is not contained in prices. As a consequence, the parties to a transaction may each possess some private information that they either cannot or will not transfer to the other. This situation will effect the market outcome and may in fact lead to certain markets not coming into being. Two interesting applications of this work are: Akerlof (1970) and Rothschild and Stiglitz (1976).

17 It is common here to see discussion of the supposed trade-off between efficiency and equity. This refers to the possibility that a move that may be in the interests of equity may reduce efficiency. We agree with Abelson that "contrary to popular versions of economics, policy decisions do not involve a simple trade-off between efficiency and equity, they also involve quite complex choices between various fairness criteria" (1987, p.10). It is the complexity of these latter choices that we wish to focus on. For this reason we also avoid discussion of "second-best" issues.

18 Function here refers to the relation or rule that allows us to rank outcomes in terms of the well-being of society.

19 Graff, 1957, pp. 10, 11

20 Arrow, 1973, p. 248

21 Permanent People's Tribunal, 1988, p. 16

22 Clark, 1987, p. 2

23 Musgrave, 1959, p. 60

24 Abelson, 1987, p. 6

25 Rawls, 1973, p. 323

Chapter 7

Fairness in Current Proposals

Introduction

Is there a need for policy intervention to tackle the debt crisis? Dornbusch (1988) identifies four reasons: a belief that the market cannot easily generate a solution that secures debts while ensuring development finance, and hence a better long run ability to secure debts; a concern lest there be a spillover of the debt crisis into foreign policy matters; a desire that stable, democratic institutions prosper in the debtor countries; and the trade problems of the world economy. We can add to this the concern that the unfettered operation of the market, from the prevailing set of property rights and property endowments, cannot produce an equitable solution to the debt crisis.

The task now is to illustrate how the criteria developed in Chapter 6 may be used to appraise proposals for solving the debt crisis. Our objectives are: to provide a set of questions which need to be asked of any proposal and to illustrate how the criteria outlined in Chapter 6 can be used in addressing these questions.

The most basic question concerns the case for debt reduction. This will be addressed in the following section. We find in favour of reducing debts. Next is the problem of instituting debt reduction on an equitable basis. Then we examine the approach to granting debt reduction. The next section considers how equitable debt reduction might be operationalised. Finally, in the last section we identify a number of issues that will need to be addressed in conjunction with debt reduction.

The case for debt reduction

In this section we will be concerned with the case for and against debt reduction. Most of the discussion will involve efficiency arguments but we will conclude with an examination of issues related to ability-to-pay.

One of the most common arguments against debt reduction is that it would introduce perverse moral hazard incentives. That is, in the presence of debt forgiveness, debtors who would otherwise have paid the full amount would now declare themselves unable or unwilling to pay. Under these circumstances, it is virtually impossible to distinguish genuine from opportunistic hardship. This is basically the argument that under debt forgiveness the market outcome would not be efficient.

It is also argued that debt forgiveness in the current period could lead to expectations that similar conditions would prevail in the future. If this was the case, creditors could believe that there would be a higher proportion of poor quality debtors in the market and as a consequence they would charge higher lending rates to cover the perceived risk. Even more important, access to credit markets might be affected in the future thereby leading to a short term solution at the cost of a longer term problem. However, there may be a sense in which this point of view is overly pessimistic. For instance, the experience of debtor countries in the 1930s suggested that failure to pay loans did not necessarily result in a subsequent denial of access to credit markets, nor was the reverse the case – countries which did repay loans were subsequently denied access to credit markets.

There is also the argument that there is no such thing as a free lunch so that someone other than the debtors will be taking a loss. Individuals in developed countries would bear the loss either as shareholders of the creditor banks, or as taxpayers should the loss be absorbed by the governments or official agencies funded by the developed world.

The general case for debt forgiveness derives from concern over the current outflow of resources from the developing world. This outflow was in fact aggravated rather than alleviated in the aftermath of the Baker Plan and indeed the failure of the Baker Plan highlights this point. The belief is that this outflow is unsustainable in terms of either financial resources or political stability. A number of considerations are cited as evidence for this view: the growing political strife in Latin American countries; the continued failure for growth to re-emerge in the developing world; the almost devastated condition of many low-income countries; and the deprivation of basic needs as documented by UNICEF (1987).

The efficiency case for debt forgiveness is made on two interrelated grounds: the debt overhang and the debt-Laffer Curve. The size of external obligations which hangs over debtor countries in the Third World has been extensively documented in Chapter 2. We have also seen that the outcomes in terms of growth and investment have been poor since 1982. The "debt overhang hypothesis" argues that this debt burden has caused the poor economic performance in highly indebted countries.

Two main channels have been identified through which the debt overhang reduces economic efficiency. First, large debt-service payments give rise to high tax rates which discourage capital formation and the repatriation of capital flight. Debt-service obligations themselves act as a tax on improved perform-ance. That is, if the value of exports increase, a part of the additional resources may have to be used to service the debt.[1] Therefore the debtor only shares partially in any increase in output. This can lower the perceived return to investment for the debtor and lower investment in the private sector even when the debt is held by the government. Second, since the government is the primary maker of payments in most debtor countries and since payments figure in its budget, they can prevent a devaluation which would improve the trade balance. Their incentive to do this results from the fact that a devaluation would increase the domestic currency cost of servicing foreign debt denominated in foreign currencies. This would increase the budget deficit, raise the money supply and fuel inflation. Hence, other less efficient methods will be sought to create a trade surplus (Kenen, 1990). Proponents of this view among economists have included, Rudiger Dornbusch and Paul Krugman of MIT, Jeffrey Sachs of Harvard and Peter Kenen of Princeton.

This view is disputed by other economists, however. Jeremy Bulow of Stanford and Ken Rogoff of Berkley (1990) argue that the debt problem is best viewed as a symptom of poor growth rather than its primary cause. The problem of resolving dispute is difficult as at a theoretical level it involves distinguishing between the major determinants of the drop in investment. For instance, if the drop in investment has been a result of weak capital inflows, a reduction in the stock of debt without a large change in current net capital flows would not be expected to increase investment substantially, since the debt reduction would not increase the supply of foreign savings to the debtor country or reduce domestic real interest rates (IMF, 1989).

It is necessary therefore to make an evaluation of the "debt overhang" case on the basis of actual empirical evidence. There has not been extensive research on this issue to date, however. What evidence does exist suggests that the "debt overhang" hypothesis cannot eassily be dismissed (IMF, 1989). In comparing countries with and without debt-servicing problems, the former group is seen to have experienced relatively severe drops in investment-output ratios. The question then arises as to whether this investment fall explains the growth slowdown. IMF calculations suggest that the decline in investment accounts for less than half of the growth shortfall. Much of the remaining causal factors may themselves be complementary to the debt overhang, however.

On the basis of this preliminary evidence the "debt overhang hypothesis" must be taken seriously. It suggests that debt reduction may be efficiency enhancing. In a situation where policy cannot await further research the best policy advice would be that debt reduction is worth trying on efficiency grounds.

Related to the "debt overhang hypothesis" is the notion of a Debt Relief Laffer Curve.[2] The idea here is that when external debt for a country becomes very large the present discounted value of repayments that the creditor can expect falls. The reason for this is summarised by Kenen as follows: "The income-depressing effects of the debt make it more likely that the debtor will default when an adverse shock arives. By reducing that vunerability, debt relief raises the *expected value of the debt*" (our emphasis).[3]

The argument made by Kenen in favour of this view is not based on the presence of a debt overhang as such. Instead he suggests that the Debt Laffer Curve comes into being because debt reduction may tilt the debtor's cost-benefit calculation against repudiation. That is, debt reduction has the effect of increasing the present value of the penalties relative to the benefits from debt repudiation. In this sense debt reduction is efficiency enhancing because it results in potential benefits for debtor and creditor alike – the debtor has less to pay now and the creditor can expect to receive more overall. In the language of our discussion in Chapter 6 it holds up the possibility of a Pareto improving move.

This argument is highly tentative. It certainly does not enjoy widespread suppport among economists. While the analysis is interesting and may very well be accurate there is no evidence to support the argument. That is, no one has actually calculated a Debt Laffer Curve for any debtor country. Even the proponents of the view differ on its applicability. Paul Krugman of MIT feels that small debtors are on the downward sloping side of the curve – the area where debt reduction is efficiency enhancing. He is not sure where to place the large debtors. On the other hand, Peter Kenen believes that large debtors are more likely on the downward sloping side. On its own, this argument, as it currently stands, would not be sufficient to merit advocacy of debt reduction. However, it is a useful supplement to the "debt overhang hypothesis". Overall then there does seem to be a reasonable efficiency case for debt reduction.

Can a case for debt reduction be made on the grounds of ability-to-pay? This type of argument could certainly be persuasive in the case of Sub-Saharan African debtors. However, in the case of Latin American countries, objections can be raised. Bulow and Rogoff (1990) point out that average per capita income in the 17 highly indebted countries was $1430 in 1987 compared to $470 in developing East Asia and $290 in South Asia. Across the board debt reduction could therefore induce inequity. Better-off developing countries could be made even better-off. This would certainly be exacerbated where officially backed debt reduction served to reduce aid received by low-income countries. On a within-country basis this could give rise to regressive income transfers. To the extent that income is less evenly distributed in Latin America than in Asia, debt reduction that impaired aid could result in improvements for the better-off in Latin American countries. Bulow and Rogoff summarise their argument forcibly: "Fundamentally, decisions about where to provide foreign aid in the 1990s should not be straightjacketed by the decisions commercial bank lending officers made in the 1970s. Why should wealthy Brazil, which borrowed to finance pharaonic investments in the 1970s, receive scarce aid funds that might otherwise go to poor but growing Thailand or impoverished Africa?".4

These authors may overstate their argument somewhat. However, they make an important point. Even accepting an efficiency case for debt reduction – as we do – we must be aware that on ability-to-pay grounds the method of debt reduction will need to be fair across developing countries. The message we take from Bulow and Rogoff is that ability-to-pay is not a strong basis for debt reduction. If there are to be transfers from the developed world there are more urgent cases to be considered before Latin America. Some might argue that all should be aided. This is fine if there is no budget constraint. However, there is a limited amount that will be transferred in practice.[5] Care must therefore be taken lest an officially backed debt reduction programme gives rise to aid being siphoned away from low-income towards middle-income countries.[6]

Approach to debt reduction

Debt reduction is now firmly on the agenda in the wake of the 1989 Brady initiative. This does not mean that debt will be effectively reduced or that the debt problem will be "solved". Neither, of course, does it ensure that any debt reduction will proceed fairly. The approach that forms the basis of agreements will determine the effectiveness and equity of any debt reduction.

A number of issues have been debated in regard to this approach. These relate to whether debt reduction should: proceed on a voluntary or mandatory basis; whether a case-by-case or a comprehensive approach is appropriate; and whether conditionality is required and, if so, of what nature.

Williamson (1988) has made a virtue of the idea of voluntary debt reduction. The meaning of voluntary seems to be that creditor banks should not be coerced into some agreement. Should this occur, it is feared that the return to normal lending would subsequently be delayed. This point is one that emerges again and again in the eight years of the debt crisis. In the light of the defaults of the 1930s and the banks' subsequent willingness to lend, it is surprising that this issue is taken at all seriously.

The notion of voluntary participation seems to us to be illusory. Commercial banks have responded when they have been forced to do so. In Chapter 4 we saw that, at the begining of the debt crisis, the IMF threatened not to disburse funds unless the banks continued to lend. This tradition has continued. It is fairly clear that US government pressure "behind the scenes" was important for the conclusion of the July 1989 Mexican deal with its creditor banks.

In addition the incentive for US banks to grant loans to Latin American countries derived in large part from the passing of the US Foreign Immunities Act of 1976. This Act exempted the commercial activities of a government, including sovereign borrowing, from sovereign immunity. As a consequence it would have been reasonable for commercial banks to conclude that sovereign debtors would not have been immune from sanctions in US courts in the event of failure to meet conditions in an

Third World Debt : Towards an Equitable Solution

agreement. Experience suggests that US courts have not been prepared to enforce a creditor's claim against sovereign borrowers when this has been deemed to be contrary to national interest by the US government (Eaton, 1990).

Therefore we do not face a choice between voluntary and mandatory. Any solution will be what we might call indicative. The challenge for those seeking a solution – and here we must be pragmatic and recognise that this will have to be the leading industrial nations – is to fix on an appropriate solution and then devise a means of inducing creditors and debtors to move towards this solution.

The next issue concerns whether a plan should be comprehensive/global or case-by-case. While the terms global and case-by-case enjoy universal usage, it is not entirely clear what these terms mean. A useful distinction is one where all terms and conditions of a solution are to apply to all debtors and creditors (global) or only to a subset (case-by-case).

The basic argument against a global solution is that it would be informationally-inefficient. Since it imposes a plan devised by some person/agency, it denies the possibility for a better solution to emerge from the interaction of creditors and debtors. Furthermore, there is the question as to whether a global plan would be operationally credible given that the viability of a scheme will depend on economic and political realities. Therefore global schemes would appear to be inefficient in that they allow no scope for choice and consequently the possibility of making mutually advantageous improvements.

A global plan would be not be equitable to the extent that it did not recognise differences between countries. Equity aside there is the practical issue that the composition of debt differs dramatically between middle-income debtors and the Sub-Saharan countries.

As was mentioned above, we do envisage that a solution be devised. Some parameters need to be set for debt reduction schemes. However, a global plan which cannot be tailored to particular circumstances is neither practical nor desirable.

Finally we come to the question of conditionality. To the extent that a solution to the debt problem is to be case-by-case, a method of ranking countries for debt forgiveness (or a degree thereof) is required. In the past, conditionality has been linked to market based economic performance measures – for example, inflation and exchange rate targets. These types of conditions are important. However, their achievement may not prevent deprivation occurring on a large scale. Concentration on these conditions may reflect a simplistic presumption that the market performs the same role in all social systems. Social choices are made by a combination of mechanisms including voting systems, customs and the market (Arrow, 1963). The same mix will not be present in all countries. Rawls' criterion of liberty might be used to argue that conditionality should respect such differences between social systems. The problem then is to come up with a set of conditions that will be useful in guiding a country towards an economically sustainable solution while respecting basic liberties.

Economic sustainability will require certain conditions and we will discuss these further in the next section. But what about conditions that are directed towards ensuring the provision of basic needs for a population? We might refer to these as welfare conditions. This poses great difficulties. We certainly have no easy solution. The most fundamental difficulty is brought out by the following example. Consider the most extreme form of deprivation, a famine. In the past the developed world has intervened in such circumstances by shipping emergency food and medical supplies to the stricken areas. Such aid, while generally welcome, has often given rise to conflict between the domestic government and the providers of aid. The conceptual problem we are attempting to highlight is this: should welfare criteria be left to the government of a country or is this something that should be explicit in a debt reduction scheme? In terms of our criteria, does liberty say that we should respect the views of the government or should we instead be concerned with the subsistence needs of the people? We believe that, in view of the major inequities in income distributions in developing countries, a debt reduction scheme must contain conditions related to basic subsistence. Otherwise, taking income distributions as historical evidence, debt relief may not directly benefit the least well-off.

One way of taking account of basic needs would be to use indices of subsistence (for example, the extent of malnutrition among children or more generally the information gathered by UNICEF in its study of the plight of children in the Third World). The Human Development Index (HDI) compiled by the United Nations might be ideal for this purpose. Such an index would be used to determine initial ability-to-pay. For instance, of two countries with similar debt service scenarios, the one with a poorer index of subsistence would receive priority. Since an index of subsistence is not immediately under the control of the country's government, the potential for moral hazard problems is reduced. Similarly the objections concerning inter-debtor equity are attenuated to the extent that forgiveness is related to ability to pay under such a scheme.

One of the long-run objectives of debt forgiveness would be to improve such an index. In the short-term a means of monitoring progress in this direction would be required. Targets for spending on health and education might be a way of doing this. This monitoring role might be invested with the UN/WHO just as the World Bank/IMF act as monitors on other conditions. What we envisage, however, is a general monitoring committee containing members of each of these organisations. The exact role of such a committee will be described in the next section.

Implementation of debt reduction

In this section we outline the means we consider appropriate for achieving an equitable solution to the debt problem. The solution we envisage involves debt reduction as we mentioned earlier. Here we will be concerned with the mechanics of a solution.

The mechanics of debt reduction involve a number of issues. At the general level there is the need to distinguish between debt owed to commercial banks and that owed to official sources. We begin with official debt. This study has been biased towards considering the question of commercial debt. In this, it reflects the preoccupation of much of the debate, especially among economists, about the debt problem. The tendency to neglect consideration of official debt stems, we believe, from the acceptance that the low-income countries who are primarily indebted to official sources are insolvent. The need for the write-off of these debts seems to be overwhelming. Commentators such as Feldstein et al (1987), while stopping short of proposing debt reduction for middle-income countries, share this view.

In the light of this consensus, it is disappointing that progress in the direction of writing-off official debt for low-income countries has been so slow. This stems in large part from difficulties in reducing bilateral official aid and the question of whether it is within the charter of multilateral agencies to write-off debt. Some progress on bilateral debt has been made with the Toronto Terms. However, as the World Bank (1989) points out, a lot more needs to be done. In addition, low-income countries outside of Africa are often exempt from IMF/World Bank sponsored programmes. It is important that these not be forgotten. Apart from suggesting that popular pressure continue to monitor progess on these issues we have nothing to add in this area.

Our main focus is on the mechanics of reducing debt which is owed to commercial banks. In our opinion the debate reduces to three questions: Is there a need for a debt reduction facility? Is there a role for the use of secondary markets? Is there a need for some form of interest capping?

As we saw in Chapter 4, a number of the solutions that have been proposed for the resolution of the debt problem have involved the creation of a new intermediary agency. For instance, the plans of Kenen (1983 and 1990), Rohatyn (1983) and Soros (1984) involve the creation of some third party agency distinct from the IMF/World Bank.

The case for a new agency is that it would be a facilitator of a settlement. Sachs (1990) likens it to a bankruptcy court. Bulow and Rogoff,[7] however, reject the idea that a new agency would facilitate an agreement between a debtor and its creditors. They suggest that the presence of such an agency would make creditors and debtors intransigent in their posture. Moreover they believe that the agency would end up bearing some of the burden of debt reduction. They illustrate their argument with an example. A house owner wishes to sell his house and asks for a price of £55,000. The only person interested in buying offers £45,000. On their own they might quickly reach a settlement of, say, £50,000. If a real estate agent was involved, they might each become more intransigent and it might be necessary for the agent to kick-in some of her fee in order to secure a deal.

The Bulow and Rogoff example is appropriate for a case of three way bargaining. That is, each of the parties seeks to gain from an agreement. An agency, as we understand it, would be directed towards setting the "rules of the game". Therefore we do not accept their argument as being persuasive in this context.

The main issue is whether coordination can occur without an agency. It might. However, the fact is that agencies are already involved. The Brady initiative – a so-called voluntary programme – explicitly involves the IMF/World Bank. It is not then a question of leaving debtors and creditors to their own devices in bargaining but rather what type of agency should be involved and what its functions ought to be.

The agency we envisage would be a Coordination Committee. Its main function would be to set the parameters for bargaining. In particular these parameters would involve conditionality that involved equity criteria. It could, for example, be comprised of officers seconded from the IMF, World Bank, UN and WHO.

The purpose of secondment would be to draw the relevant expertise together and also to signal that its existence would be temporary. It could be headed by a non-agency person, possibly from the academic or business community.

It would be important that the agency play as limited a role as possible. Here we should mention that Sachs (1988) himself observed that solutions to the 1930s debt crisis were more often reached by one-on-one negotiation between creditor and debtor rather than through intermediation through a third party. The fact that debtors had repudiated may have facilitated this development.

We therefore agree with Kenen, Sachs and others who call for some sort of debt facility. We prefer to call it a Coordination Committee. The reason for this is that we do not believe, as they do, that the facility should guarantee interest payments. We find it difficult to accept their advocacy of a guarantee especially when they are the very people who believe that there exists a Debt Laffer Curve. If it exists, then the failure to resolve the debt problem is a coordination failure. Establishing an agency with some sort of power to force coordination – we will discuss such powers below – should then be sufficient. If this does not suceed then there is no debt overhang and then it is time enough to talk about interest guarantees.[8]

Kenen (1990) would probably counter along the lines that he criticises the Brady initiative. That is, he says that the Brady proposal does not go far enough: it relies too heavily on debtors and creditors to reach mutually beneficial bargains; it does not shift risk sufficiently from private to official creditors; and it fails to provide sufficient resources to achieve the needed debt reduction. We share his dissatisfaction with the Brady Plan. However, we do not agree with his reasons. In the first place if secondary market prices are any guide then there is plenty of room for mutually advantageous gains from bilateral bargains. Secondly we are dubious about the efficacy of shifting risk from private to official creditors. Doing this is to place the agencies in the three way bargaining situation that Bulow and Rogoff examine. Finally, as was argued in the previous section, we believe that resources made available for aid should be distributed separately from the debt reduction process.

We must be fair to Sachs (1990) and mention that he does recognise the apparent inconsistency in his argument. He believes that guarantees are necessary: to give the agency a firm legal basis for imposing settlements; to protect the banks against the fear that they will be pressured by their governments to give more relief in the future; and to force public sharing of the burden of debt reduction. Again we would oppose the third reason on the grounds mentioned above. As regards the first reason, we acccept that the agency might have problem in enforcement but we do not believe that a guarantee is the means of solving this problem. The second issue is a genuine concern. A guarantee would certainly help in making assurances to the creditors credible. However, we believe that this on its own is not a sufficient basis for a guarantee.

Ought the secondary market be used in debt reduction? We believe that there is a role for secondary markets. However, it is not the role advocated since the emergence of debt-equity swaps in the mid 1980s. There is now fairly wide agreement that the debt-equity swap is not a panacea for the debt problem. The inflationary consequences alone make this an undesirable option. The World Bank (1989) endorses this view and reports a major downturn in secondary market activity in 1989.

A recent development in the secondary market is the increasing number of buybacks, exit-bonds and informal conversions – the latter consisting of conversions by private citizens and companies. As we said in Chapter 4, it is basically the market means of buying out of involuntary lending. There is nothing intrinsically wrong here. However, the benefits that countries can expect are very small.

In the case of the July 1989 Mexican deal, Kenen (1990) calculates, on the assumption that sixty per cent of banks take the exit-bonds (which is optimistic), that the face value of debt will be cut by only sixteen per cent! If debt reduction is this meagre the relief may not be enough to revitalise the economy. As a consequence their ability to service payments on these bonds may be threatened. Then the official guarantees will be called. We will be back where we started except that official agencies will have purchased the claims on debtors at prices well above those prevailing in the current secondary amrket.

In our opinion the most suitable role for secondary markets is the one for which they were originally conceived – to facilitate inter-bank transactions. If banks wish to reduce their exposure to debtor countries, let them sell their claim to other banks. The participation by others may actually raise secondary market prices. In addition we see the secondary market as providing a guide to the Coordination Committee for the extent of debt reduction that seems appropriate.

A solution is needed to reduce debt service to debtors now and at the same time give the banks good reason for believing that payments will continue to be made in the future. The most straightforward way of doing this is to reduce interest to sub-market levels on existing debt. The advantages to this means of debt service reduction are numerous: it is administratively straightforward; it is equitable across banks dealing with a particular country; it is the means generally used in dealing with poor debt domestically; and, in the US context, it has advantages in regard to bank regulations. The saving for debtors should be capitalised and applied to investment in the domestic economy.

The use of capitalised savings would be monitored by the coordinating committee. Such use would be subject to conditionality. The most basic condition would be that the funds could not be transferred out of the country. There is room for some variation here in that creditors could accept lower foreign currency payments in return for some payments in domestic currency. This is along the lines of Dornbusch's (1988) interest re-cycling proposal. Again any payments in domestic currency could not be transferred out of the debtor country.

The nature of conditionality would involve economic and welfare performance criteria. The economic criteria would be along the lines suggested by Dornbusch (1988): legislative reform to overcome nationalism and pave the way for domestic and foreign investment; and major budget reform – involving tax reform and expenditure programme monitoring. The IMF/World Bank representatives on the committee would be principally responsible for monitoring such progress – in practice, of course, actual analysis would need to be contracted out.

The welfare criteria would involve targets for spending on health and education. The exact details here would be a matter to be agreed based on the expertise of the UN and WHO in this area.

For the debtors the advantage would be that resources are freed up immediately to redress the debt overhang problem. This would translate into benefits for the creditors in terms of enhanced payments prospects. Banks wishing to withdraw from the process would have the option of selling off their claims to other banks on the secondary market.

But will bargaining take place? In the first instance the slimming of the menu of options for debt reduction will, we believe, help. This will preclude unnecessary debate and haggling. The committee will also need a stick to force the debtors and creditors to the bargaining table – the following is an illustration of how this might be done. In relation to the debtors, they would initially be told to pay some reduced level of service into a trust fund administered by the committee. The actual amount for any debtor would be calculated on the basis of historic prices on the secondary market. This amount would be greater than the actual payments that would be envisioned after an agreement with creditors. Failure to make payments would be followed by trade credit restrictions. Pending the completion of an agreement the creditors would receive no payments. Hence they have an incentive to come to the bargaining table. In order to avoid disruption a six month grace period could be given before this process is put in place. Hence creditors would have an incentive to bargain in advance of re-routing of payments to the committee.

What about the equity of such a scheme? The committee would in the process described above, be setting the limits on the range of debt reduction. Depending on the current secondary market prices, this range would obviously differ between countries. However, the committee should also be guided by welfare criteria in setting the range above current market prices. Such prices would merely be indicative. The purpose here is to avoid conferring benefits to relatively well-off but indigent debtors.

Ability-to-pay considerations enter in the setting of ranges. Horizontial equity would play a role in determining whether the committee would ratify an agreement. The task here would be to ensure that debtors in similar circumstances are treated in a similar way.

It would be up to creditor banks to organise themselves for bargaining with debtors. The free-rider problem would be solved because any banks not cooperating with their partners would have very little possibility of payment.

Depending on market conditions, debtors may experience difficulties in meeting future payments. This possibility should be recognised in any agreement and agreed contingent terms should exist for such situations. The contingencies could be based on indicators such as the terms of trade.

Clearly the initial agreements would involve considerable bargaining. However, we envision that some sort of a model agreement would in time emerge. This would leave only the details of a particular case to be agreed.

The financing role of industrialised countries would be limited to paying for the operation of the Coordination Committee.

Future considerations

In the future the question of new sources of foreign money will be an important consideration. We believe that changes in bank regulations in developed countries are fundamental. In the first instance these changes are necessary in order to tackle the problem of capital flight. The issue of capital flight was mentioned in Chapter 4. Estimates for capital flight differ widely as noted by Williamson and Lesard (1987). Morgan Guaranty estimate capital flight from Argentina, Brazil, Mexico and Venezuela between 1976 and 1984 to be of the order of $125 billion while Williamson and Lessard's preferred measure is $82 billion.

More recently, Bulow and Rogoff (1990) estimate that Latin American bank deposits alone, of the group of seventeen highly indebted countries, lodged with banks in the developed world are about equal to the secondary market value of claims on these countries. Two issues arise in dealing with the capital flight problem. One concerns future capital flight. Restrictions on withdrawing savings from debt service reductions and a better climate for investment are vital in this regard.

The second issue concerns the historical stock of capital flight. Some incentives need to be given for the return of this capital. A better climate for investment in the domestic country is again important. In addition, the US should tax Latin American deposits held in their banks.

The reform of US banking regulations is an issue that goes beyond the scope of this study. However, a number of commentators suggest that the conditions which encouraged US bank lending in the 1970s should be re-examined. Bulow and Rogoff (1990) go as far as suggesting that adjudication on debtor-country loans should be directed towards the courts in these countries. At any rate we believe that a review of these issues is important.

The final point we wish to draw attention to is what we consider to be an important trend in the development of economic relations between countries. We are referring here to the growth of federations. The evolution of the EU is the obvious example. Countries within this federation are moving towards freer trade while putting mechanisms for income transfer between regions in place. The North American Free Trade Agreement is contributing towards the growth of a larger trading block. In the future we should expect Eastern European countries to evolve towards a federal relationship between sovereign states. Such a development might also be a means of resolving current tensions within OPEC. This last point is obviously quite speculative. In Asia the obvious focus for federalism is Japan.

If such federalism is to develop, we will see a growth in regional free trade. The trade relations between federal blocks is harder to predict. However, it is fair to say that we could see some form of "strategic trade policy" evolving. This then raises the question of what blocks will include the current debt-distressed countries. For Latin America there is already some signs that the US sees the future as involving some more concrete economic relations with them. President Bush's "Enterprise for the Americas Initiative", announced in June 1990, is an indication of the direction of future policy. While it is fanciful to make comparisons with the European Union, the issue does concede that the US recognises economic interdependance.

For low-income African debtors the development of federalism raises the problem of association. There are no obvious economic allies. The Lomé process might be extended in such a way as to strengthen the link with the EU.[9] However, Eastern Europe seems to be a greater concern to the EU at the moment. Therefore, the low-income countries in Africa not only face severe problems with debt now but they may find that the development of trade blocks will present them with problems in the future. We therefore conclude with a point made earlier. An equitable solution must ensure that future aid policy will not be threatened by policies designed to reduce debt for middle-income debtors.

Footnotes

1   Eaton (1990) disputes the extent to which this is the case in practice. Clearly the actual amount of debt payments will be a function of specific negotiations between creditors and debtors. The IMF (1989) believe, however, that the statement in the text is qualitatively accurate in general.

2   This is an unfortunate name but we shall stick with it as it has enjoyed widespread use in the literature.

3   Kenen, 1990, p. 10

4   Bulow and Rogoff, 1990, p. 38

5   This is not to dismiss the argument for giving more aid. Rather it is a recognition that the actual trends have not been in this direction and that pragmatic policy must operate from current conditions.

6   This argument could be extended to discuss the general issue of how to treat poor countries that did not borrow relative to those that did. Some, especially those using a process view of justice might argue that the debtors must be punished. We are in no way making such an argument. Rather we are

cautioning against an unintended consequence of policy. That is, care must be taken lest a package designed to help debtors results in unintended deprivation for non-debt distressed countries which could occur if there is, in practice, an aid budget constraint.

7   Bulow and Rugoff, 1990. This example is more relevant in North America where real estate agents take a larger percentage share than in Ireland. The example they use is not an uncommon event in the US.

8   If there is a Debt Laffer Curve then mutually advantageous gains can be made by debtors and creditors from debt reduction. This should be compensation enough for each side.

9   This would obviously involve considerable change in the composition of Lomé countries and the actual links they have with the European Union's structures.

Chapter 8

Recommendations

This Chapter contains a listing of our recommendations in point form. It is intended as a summary. Readers seeking more detail should refer to Chapter 7.

(1) A case for debt reduction can be made on the basis of economic efficiency. The central element of this case is the "debt overhang hypothesis". This suggests that poor economic outcomes in debtor countries are caused, at least in part, by the large scale of debt which hangs over these countries. When debt service is "excessive" the returns to productive investment are reduced. This discourages capital formation and halts growth. The debt service effectively acts as a tax on growth in the debtor countries. Reducing debt service will make the debtor better-off. It will also enhance the prospects for growth and, all other things being equal, improve the payment prospects of creditors.

(2) An efficiency case for debt reduction can also be made on the basis of a Debt Laffer Curve. This is the suggestion that debt reduction can increase the expected stream of payments for creditors by tilting the debtors cost/benefit calculation against default. Again debt reduction improves the lot of creditors and debtors. We are somewhat sceptical about this argument because, unlike the debt overhang hypothesis, there is no empirical evidence to support the claim. However, we do accept that it is a possibility.

(3) In assessing schemes for debt reduction, we employ a number of criteria of equity in addition to that of efficiency mentioned above. These are derived from what we call the "outcome" view of justice. Arguments relating to this choice are presented in Chapter 6. The full set of criteria are: liberty; efficiency; vertical equity; and horizontial equity.

(4) We consider that arguments for debt reduction made on the basis of vertical equity suggest that care must be exercised by official agencies lest their involvement in debt reduction leads, in effect, to the re-routing of aid from low-income to middle-income countries.

(5) We consider debate about voluntary versus mandatory debt reduction to be irrelevent. Schemes that are considered voluntary have always involved some element of pressure on creditor banks. They are in this sense what we call indicative. We favour a clearer recognition of this so that debate can more fruitfully centre around the indications given to creditors and debtors.

(6) A completely global solution to the debt crisis is not practical. However, some indication of the broad parameters of all agreements must be established on a universal basis. Details concerning, in particular, the extent of debt reduction must be carried-out on a case-by-case basis.

(7) In order to tackle debt owed to commercial banks, a Coordination Committee should be established. This committee ought to be staffed by representatives from the IMF, World Bank, UN, and the World Health Organization. Its operation should be funded by the governments of industrial countries. The role of the committee would be to encourage debtors and creditors to agree to debt reduction. The means of debt reduction should be limited to the reduction of interest rates on debt below market levels. On the basis of secondary market prices and human welfare indicators the committee would establish the range for debt reduction. The committe would be charged with the function of ensuring that there was no discrimination in terms of the conditions offered to debtors on the basis of irrelevent characteristics. Debt reduction would be subject to conditionality which would be monitored by the committee. Such conditionality would include economic and human welfare criteria. No guarantees from official sources would be used to back any agreements. The power of the committee should derive from a declaration that debt service be directed to the committee in advance of agreements. The committee should use sanctions such as the blocking of trade credits against debtors who fail to make such payments. Of course there is nothing stopping debtors from staying outside the process. The prospect of better terms should induce most debtors to participate, however. Creditors will have an incentive to move towards quick agreement in order to get payments. To avoid disruption a grace period could be declared in which agreements could be brought forward before debt service is re-routed to the committee. In a sense this proposal involves a kind of "managed repudiation".

(8) We suggest that use of the secondary markets for debt be limited to inter-bank transactions, which is the purpose for which they originally developed.

(9) In order to provide an environment in which financial relations between banks and developing countries can return to a normal working basis we believe that a review of banking legislation, especially in the US, is urgently required. As part of this some attention must be given to the question of capital flight. The taxation of Latin American deposits in industrial country banks is a means of reducing the relative attractiveness of capital flight. Of course, improvement in the conditions for investment in the debtor countries is also a prerequisite. The question of the appropriate means of taxing internationally mobile capital is now the subject of much discussion between developed countries. The lessons from any findings here must be considered in relation to capital flight.

(10) In regard to the debt problems of the low-income countries, we believe that action to write-off official debts must continue. In particular pressure should be brought to bear on OPEC and East European countries to follow the example of OECD countries in regard to bilateral aid.

Appendix I

Main sources of international statistics on external Third World debt

We consider two source types: 1. sources with an on-going commitment to provide detailed external debt and debt-related statistics on a regular basis at periodic intervals; and 2. sources which provide specific data on external debt on an occasional basis or summary of debt-related statistics on a regular basis.

1. The main sources in this category are the Bank of International Settlements (BIS), the International Monetary Fund (IMF), the Organization for Economic Co-operation and Development (OECD) and the World Bank.

    The BIS, located in Basle, Switzerland, issues a quarterly publication called *International Banking Developments*, which provides information on international bank lending by the commercial banks in the major industrial countries since 1973. The currency denominations of the loans are specific and figures adjusted for changes in the exchange rate are published for certain country groupings and for individual countries. The published data include both short-term and long-term debt but debt owed to creditors other than commercial banks is not included. Semi-annual statistics are also published by the BIS in *The Maturity Distribution of International Bank Lending*. These half-yearly data cover the total bank debt of a country as well as the principal repayments of bank debt falling due in the current year and the undisbursed existing credit commitments available to the countries.

    The IMF issues a monthly publication called *International Financial Statistics* (IFS), which provides information on the balance of payments and the foreign exchange and gold reserves of its 151 member countries and some other nations. The Fund's *International Capital Markets*, an annual study, provides flow statistics on international bank lending and deposit-taking. Further data are presented in the *World Economic Outlook*, a survey by the staff of the IMF, published annually with occasional updates. This carries statistics on external debt and debt service, as well as other macroeconomic indicators, for specific country groupings based on geographical region, predominant export, financial miscellaneous economic criteria.

The OECD publishes monthly data on bond issues and bank loans by country in its *Financial Statistics Monthly*, while data on the terms of bank lending and new external bank credit commitments are published in its *Financial Market Trends*. The former figures relate only to gross borrowings and make no allowance for repayments. The latter data provide details on medium-term and long-term gross credit commitments with a maturity exceeding one year, disaggregated into foreign and Euro-credits. Another publication of the OECD, *External Debt of Developing Countries* (Annual Survey), begun in 1985, presents detailed information from 1975 onwards on disbursed short-term and long-term debt and debt service by source and terms of lending for selected countries and country groupings. Military debt financed by official credits and debt owed to the IMF are excluded from these figures. Data are also provided in the latter publication on multilateral official debt-relief operations. In a six-monthly publication called *Statistics on External Indebtedness: Bank and Trade-Related Nonbank External Claims on Individual Borrowing Countries and Territories*, the OECD combines BIS data on bank claims and its own data on long and short-term official and guaranteed trade credits. This BIS-OECD publication also provides estimates of the guaranteed debt owed to the OECD bank and non-bank institutions. The OECD also publishes *Development Co-operation*, the annual report of the Chairman of the Development Assistance Committee (DAC). This includes detailed information on financial resource flows from DAC countries to developing countries and the multilateral agencies. Less detailed information is provided on resource flows from Arab and Council for Mutual Economic Assistance (CMEA) countries to the developing world.

The World Bank compiles data on public and publically-guaranteed long-term debt (i.e. debt with maturity exceeding one year) and debt service payments for most developing countries through its debtor reporting system (DRS). These figures are based on reports from 107 debtor countries on an annual basis. Time series data start in 1970 for most countries and in 1958 for some countries. Data on long-term private non-guaranteed debt are now provided for approximately 50 countries. This is important since it constitutes a large share of the total external debt burden in many countries. The DRS also produces data on debt structure, including average interest rates, maturities, grace periods, grant elements, undisbursed and disbursed outstanding debt, disbursements, commitments, principal debt ratios and projected debt service payments as well as loan-by-loan details. Where the issue of confidentiality does not arise, informal data on short-term debt are generated from the missions sent by the World Bank and IMF to specific developing countries. However, data on short-term debt remain deficient and further data inadequacies arise from incomplete reporting to the DRS, particularly in the case of debt arising from military expenditures. Summary statistics from the DRS are published annually in the *World Debt Tables*. This organises the information by country groupings and individual countries within each group for official creditors (bilateral and multilateral) and private creditors (financial markets, suppliers and other sources).

The main problem with the external debt statistics from the above sources is that they are not comparable. In general, the statistics are the outcome of partial data collection systems to meet particular requirements for information on external debt. As such, the organisations lack a standardised comprehensive framework for data collection. The need for co-ordination of data collection was emphasised at the first meeting of the International Compilers' Working Group on External Debt Statistics, which took place in Washington in March 1984.

2. While the publications listed above are the major sources of statistics on external debt of the developing countries, additional but less comprehensive debt and debt-related statistics are provided in the following publications: the Annual Reports of the IDA, IFC and Regional Development Banks, the bank reviews of many commercial banks in the industrialised countries, such as the *AMEX Bank Review* and the *Midland Bank Review, Euromoney* (Trade Finance Report), *Finance and Development* (a quarterly joint publication of the IMF and World Bank), the IMF Annual Report, the IMF Occasional Paper Series, Morgan Guaranty's *World Financial Markets, The Banker, The Economist Financial Report, The Financial Times, The Institutional Investor, The Wall Street Journal*, the UN *Handbook of International Trade Statistics*, the UN *Monthly Bulletin of Statistics*, the UN *World Economic Survey*, UNCTAD's *Trade and Development Report*, the UNDP's *Performance, Policy and Prospects*, UNIDO's *Industry and Development*, the World Bank's annual *World Development Report*, and others. A new source of statistics on external debt is the Institute of International Finance (IIF). Drawing data

from many sources, including the commercial banks, the IIF prepares reports on developing economies. These reports include current estimates of the external debt of these countries as well as other macroeconomic indicators.

Appendix II

Sources of financial flows to developing countries

We are speaking here of transnational resource flows, which are the result of an extension of grants and/or loans to non-residents by governments, government agencies and multilateral organisations. Before looking at resource flows channelled through different organising bodies, a distinction should be made between such resource flows and "aid". In precise terms, only that part of the total resource flow, which may be considered to be a subsidy, is aid. Under this definition, the full amount of grants in a convertible currency may be considered as aid while the full amount of loans may not. The Development Assistance Committee (DAC), which coordinates economic assistance to developing countries on behalf of OECD/EU countries, uses the term aid to cover the contributions to multilateral agencies, government grants and official loans with a maturity greater than five years, all of which are made for primarily development purposes.

A useful framework for looking at types of resource flows is the following one, which is used by Selim (1983) and which forms the basis of the DAC reports.

A. Official Development Assistance (ODA), covering:
   (a) bilateral ODA; and
   (b) contributions to multilateral institutions

B. Other official flows (OOF), covering:
   (a) bilateral OOF; and
   (b) multilateral institutions

C. Grants by private voluntary agencies.

D. Private flows at market terms:
   (a) direct investment;
   (b) bilateral portfolio investment and other;
   (c) multilateral portfolio investment; and
   (d) export credits.

The distinction between bilateral and multilateral resource flows is a fundamental one in this analysis. Bilateral flows are those which involve a direct transfer from the source country to the recipient while multilateral flows represent those resource flows which are channelled through the various multilateral agencies, for example the World Bank, the UN specialised agencies, and the OPEC country institutions (all of which are discussed below). A distinction should also be made between concessional and non-concessional resource flows. Concessional flows include grants or loans bearing lower interest rates and longer repayment periods than would be available in private international capital markets, while loans from commercial banks with market-determined interest rates and repayment periods are non-concessional flows.

According to the DAC definition, ODA includes grants and loans undertaken by the official sector under the conditions that: (i) their main objective be "the promotion of economic development and welfare" [DAC Review, 1982, p. 171] and (ii) they involve concessional terms. In the case of a loan, the latter condition means that the loan should involve at least a 25% grant element. Examples of grants include technical assistance and food aid while loans include food aid loans, equities and other financial assets. Contributions made by the official sector to multilateral institutions include grants channelled through multilateral agencies as well as capital subscription payments to these institutions and concessional lending.

Other official flows (OOF) are those official flows which carry a grant element of less than 25%. The bilateral flows include official export credits as well as equities and other bilateral assets. Official export credits are those export credits (defined below) which are made available to exporters or foreign buyers directly by the government of the exporting country.

Foreign direct investment (FDI) occurs when a company based in one country makes an investment which involves the ownership and control of a company in another country. It is basically a package deal which usually includes the transfer of long-term finance, technological skills, and managerial and marketing experience to the host country and the remittance of equity funds and profits to the source country.

In addition to FDI, there are other forms of investment in developing countries. One of these is portfolio investment in equities. An equity is a stock whose value is quoted on public stock markets. As in the case of direct investment, the equity investor purchases a share in the profits of a private company in another country. However the investment is restricted to just that – a share in the profits of the company involving no responsibility for the control of the company. Typically such investors will own shares of this type in many companies. The idea is that the investor can reduce the risk involved by holding a diversified portfolio of such equities. Hence the name portfolio investment.

An export credit results when a foreign purchaser of exported goods and services is allowed to defer payment. Such credits are supported by the private sector and their purpose is to finance the purchase of capital goods. Private export credits may take the following forms: (i) buyers' credit; and (ii) suppliers' credit. In the case of buyer's credit, the exporter's bank or credit institution lends the buyer or his bank the required finance to make the purchase. With suppliers' credit, the exporter arranges his own refinancing. Essentially, export credits are loans, which must be used for the purchase of specific capital goods, at interest rates which are fixed and subsidised according to the limits determined by the Arrangement on Guidelines for Officially Supported Export Credit Guarantees (ECG).

The organisations which handle resource flows may be classified into the following groups:

1. OECD Organisations
2. OPEC Organisations
3. Centrally Planned Economy Organisations
4. The Multilateral Financial Institutions

1. OECD organisations

In 1959, members of the Organisation for European Economic Co-operation (OEEC) agreed to set up the Development Assistance Group (DAG) as a forum for discussing the mechanisms for and monitoring the supply of aid to developing countries by western countries. With the establishment of the OECD in 1961, the DAG was transformed into the Development Assistance Committee (DAC). Membership of the OECD and the DAC are not identical, however. The non-DAC OECD countries are Greece, Iceland, Luxembourg, Portugal and Spain.

2. The OPEC organisations

OPEC came into being in September 1960. Its members now include: Iran, Iraq, Kuwait, Saudi Arabia, Venezuela, Qatar, Indonesia, Libya, United Arab Emirates, Algeria, Nigeria, Ecuador and Gabon, with Trinidad and Tobago having observer status. For convenience the multinational Arab institutions will also be discussed here.

OPEC institutions for extending assistance to developing countries fall into two types: (i) those which are nationally based and (ii) those which are multilateral in nature. Those institutions dealing with national funds include: the Abu Dhabi Fund for Arab Economic Development (ADFAED), the Iraqi Fund for External Development (IFED), the Kuwait Fund for Arab Economic Development (KWAED), the Libyan Bank for Foreign Assistance (LBFA), and the Venezuelan Fund (VF). The multilateral institutions include: the Arab Authority for Agricultural Investment and Development (AAAID), the Arab Bank for Economic Development in Africa (ABEDA), the Arab Fund for Economic and Social Development (AFESD), the Arab Monetary Fund (AMF), the Islamic Development Bank (IDB) and the OPEC Fund for International Development (OPECFID). Apart from ADFAED, AFESD and KFAED (which came into operation before 1973), all of the above institutions were set up following the increase in oil prices in 1973, with the objective of channelling unused revenues resulting from the oil price increase to Third World countries.

The conditions, i.e. interest rates, grace periods, methods and timing of repayments, under which all of the OPEC national funds provide loans to developing countries are similar. The main differences lie in the types of activities/projects in the developing countries, which they will consider as being suitable for these loans. The same is true among the multilateral institutions. In general, the OPEC institutions operate as follows. The developing countries send a delegation to the institution to request finance for a particular project (or projects). The institution, in turn, sends a delegation, which includes international experts, to the petitioning country to evaluate the project. Once the evaluation has been completed, it is up to the board of the institution to make a decision on whether to accept or reject the project as being suitable for finance.

3. The Centrally Planned Economy Organisations

It is difficult to present a comprehensive description of the sources of flows of financial resources from the Centrally Planned Economies (CPEs) (i.e. the non-market economies of the former USSR and Eastern Europe) to the developing countries for a number of reasons. First, real developments in economic relations between the CPEs and the developing countries began in 1960 and are consequently new in comparison with the industrial countries. Second, it is difficult to get accurate statistics on resources flows, in particular bilateral flows. Third, bilateral resource flows tend to be more strongly linked to political considerations and therefore subject to changes in political policies than in the industrial countries. These circumstances do not provide a good basis for the development of an institutional structure for on-going resource flows.

The Council for Mutual Economic Assistance (CMEA/COMECON), is the main source of information on resource flows. The objective of bilateral economic assistance is to promote mutually advantageous trading conditions. Such economic assistance is tied to specific projects. Generally, resource flows take the form of loans at below-market interest rates with a grant element of 23% to 37% and commercial credits. Although both market and non-market developing countries have been the recipients of these financial flows, the terms offered to the latter group have been softer and their share in the total value of resource flows has been higher. In the past the USSR has consistently contributed the major share of bilateral resources flows.

4. The Multilateral Institutions

Multilateral financial institutions (MFIs) have played a pivotal role in the flow of financial resources to the developing world. In this section we focus on three groups of institutions: the Bretton Woods institutions, the regional banks and the UN institutions. In 1944, representatives of forty-four countries, meeting at Bretton Woods, proposed the establishment of the Bretton Woods System. The International Bank for Reconstruction and Development (IBRD), commonly called the World Bank, and the International Monetary Fund (IMF) are the remaining legacy of this proposal. In 1956, the International Finance Corporation (IFC) was established as an affiliate of the World Bank. This was followed in 1960 by a new fund, to be administered by the World Bank, in the form of the International Development Association (IDA). The regional banks for the most part represent a later development. They include the Inter-American Development Bank (IADB), set up in 1959, the African Development Bank (AfDB), set up in 1963, the Asian Development Bank (AsDB), set up in 1966 and the Caribbean Development Bank (CDB), set up in 1970. All of these institutions were designed with the objective of making loans available to their members from the capital subscriptions of the members and borrowings in the capital market. These loans would be directed towards stimulating economic growth in the developing countries.

The World Bank operates a policy of "lending for economic

development" to member countries. There is a number of steps involved in getting a loan from the World Bank. First, an assessment is made as to whether the member country is eligible to borrow from the Bank. If it is possible for the country to raise the requested finance in the private market at reasonable terms, then the country is not eligible for a loan from the Bank. Another condition for eligibility is that the country may not pursue domestic policies which adversely affect its future credit-worthiness or ability to repay the loan. Once eligibility has been confirmed, the country submits projects to the Bank for economic and financial appraisal. Accepted projects may have undergone substantial modification and strict supervision of all projects is conducted by the Bank. Loans are made only to governments or on a government guarantee. The World Bank also provides other services such as technical assistance in the form of experts to help in project preparation, short-term training courses and secondment of advisors. It also secures co-financing for projects from other multilateral institutions.

The IFC was established to fill a gap in the operations of the World Bank. The World Bank is basically a lending institution as opposed to an investment institution. This distinction is important. When a developing country incurs debt in order to finance a project, it alone, in the absence of debt default, bears the full amount of the risk of the project being financed while the lender bears no risk. Investment by a foreign company, individual or multilateral institution in an activity of another country provides a mechanism whereby part or all of the risk is transferred from the borrower to the lender. In these circumstances the foreign entity is said to be acting as a provider of risk capital. Under the Articles of the World Bank it was limited to lending to governments or on a government guarantee. So the IFC was set up to provide and mobilise risk capital for developing countries. The IFC invests in projects which it deems to be of economic benefit to the host country and to be potentially profitable. Investments are made in conjunction with others, in particular with local private enterprises. Financing is provided on commercial terms, normally at fixed rates for seven to twelve years with a grace period of two to three years.

The IDA is known as the soft loan affiliate of the World Bank. It was established as a result of a campaign by the developing countries calling for long-term, low-interest loans for economic and social development. The IDA was set up with the purpose of promoting the economic development and increased productivity of the developing country members of the World Bank. It provides interest-free loans under government guarantee for 50 years with a grace period of ten years. The distribution of resources is based on the following criteria: (1) the level of poverty in the applicant country; (2) the creditworthiness of the applicant country; (3) the economic performance of the applicant country and (4) the suitability of the proposed project(s).

The main function of the International Monetary Fund (IMF) is to supply its members with financial resources to take care of short-term balance of payments problems. The IMF accomplishes this by granting loans to its members on condition that they pursue domestic policies which will eliminate the balance of payments deficit. An individual member country's loan entitlement is determined by its quota and the total holdings of that country's currency by the IMF. A country's quota is determined by a formula based on a number of factors, including the country's national income, its foreign exchange and gold reserves and the size and variation of its foreign trade flows. Several credit facilities of the IMF, which allow countries to exceed their quotas under particular circumstances, have emerged over time to deal with specific economic events leading to balance of payments problems. Examples of such "finance windows" include: the Extended Fund Facility of 1974 and the Supplementary Financing Facility of 1979 which permitted drawings of up to 140% of the quota. Both facilities are based on a commitment by the recipient country to an economic stabilisation programme, which the IMF believes will restore its balance of payments equilibrium. This linking of credit facilities to an agreed stabilisation programme has given rise to what is called "conditionality", which is a major issue of contention between the developing countries and the IMF. Many developing countries feel that the emphasis put on internal adjustment and its stringent policing by the IMF acts as barrier rather than a means of ensuring economic growth and development. Almost all developing countries apart from some small states in the Pacific, Albania, Angola, Cuba and Taiwan are members of the IMF.

The regional banks were set up to achieve the same goal as the World Bank, namely to stimulate economic growth in developing countries. A factor in the setting up of the regional development banks was the feeling in developing countries that there needed to be a source of loans which would be extended on reasonable terms to meet particular circumstances arising in specific countries. The basic IBRD/IDA model was adopted by the regional banks. The model is one of a bank which raises money on international capital markets by selling long-term bonds. These bonds have the official backing of the member countries. The capital raised in this manner is used to cover expenses and make loans at below market rates to its members. Membership of the regional banks is open to both donor and recipient countries and voting is based on financial contribution to the institution. As in the case of the IBRD/IDA, technical assistance and policy advisers are provided in addition to financial resources.

The range of activities of the IADB spans the countries of Latin America and the Caribbean and it is based on the capital subscriptions of non-regional countries such as the US and Canada as well as 20 Caribbean and Latin American countries. The main difference between the IADB and the other regional banks is the greater volume of resources at its disposal. There is a major emphasis on agriculture in the loans extended by the bank.

The AfDB provides loans for approved development projects in its regional member countries. In an effort to mobilise further resources, the AfDB has, since 1979, allowed non-regional countries (primarily European countries and the US) to make capital subscriptions as non-regional members. Usually the bank only approves loans for 50% of the cost of the project. The bank also undertakes co-financing of projects with other international and national development institutions. The bank has in the past supported projects which would not have received World Bank approval.

The AsDB was set up as a result of the efforts of the Economic Commission for Asia and the Far East (ECAFE). It was established basically to promote investment and growth, lend funds and provide technical assistance to the developing member countries of Asia, parts of the South Pacific and the Far East. Like the AfDB, it has many non-regional members including the US. It is closer in style of operations and conditions of lending to the IBRD than any of the other regional banks.

The CDB is the smallest and newest of the regional development banks. It serves all of the Commonwealth Caribbean countries and territories and has Canada and the UK as non-regional members. Loans are extended which provide up to 80% of the cost of an approved project for the less developed member countries. As with the AfDB and AsDB, the problem of acquiring financial resources is a major one.

The core organisation for multilateral aid extended by the UN is the United Nations Development Programme (UNDP). This was set up in 1965 from a merger of the UN Expanded Programme of Technical Assistance (EPTA) and the UN Special

Fund (SF). Financial resources are built up from the voluntary contributions of the member governments of the UN. Policy guidelines are set and resource allocation decisions are made through a 48 country Governing Council of both developing and industrial countries. Participating and executive agents of the UNDP include: FAO, IBRD, IADB, ILO, UN, UNCTAD, UNESCO, UNICEF, UNIDO, WHO and others.

A Glossary of Abbreviations

AAAID	Arab Authority for Agricultural Investment and Development
ABEDA	Arab Bank for Economic Development in Africa
ACP	African, Caribbean and Pacific
ADF	African Development Fund
ADFAED	Abu Dhabi Fund for Arab Economic Development
AfDB	African Development Bank
AfDF	African Development Fund
AFESD	Arab Fund for Economic and Social Development
AID	Agency for International Development
AMF	Arab Monetary Fund
AsDB	Asian Development Bank
BIS	Bank for International Settlements
BOAD	West African Development Bank
BOP	Balance of payments
BOT	Balance of trade
CCCE	Caisse Central de Cooperation Economique
CDB	Caribbean Development Bank
CDC	Commonwealth Development Corporation
CFF	Compensatory Financing Facility
CGIAR	Consultative Group on International Agricultural Research
CIEC	Conference on International Economic Co-operation
CMEA	Council for Mutual Economic Aid
COFACE	Compagnie Francaise d'Assurance pour le Commerce Exterieur
COLTS	Continuously offered longer-term securities
CPE	Centrally Planned Economy
CPI	Consumer price index
DAC	Development Assistance Committee
DAG	Development Assistance Group
DANIDA	Danish International Development Agency
DEG	Deutsche Entwichlungsgesellshaft
DFI	Development Finance Institutions
DOM	Departements d'Outre-Mer
ECA	Economic Commission for Africa
ECAFE	Economic Commission for Asia and the Far East
ECGD	Export Credits Guarantee Department
EDF	European Development Fund
EDI	Economic Development Institute

EEC	European Economic Community
EFF	Extended Fund Facility
EIB	European Investment Bank
EKN	Swedish Export Credits Guarantee Board
EMS	European Monetary System
EPTA	Expanded Programme for Technical Assistance
ESAF	Enhanced Structural Adjustment Facility
ESCAP	Economic and Social Commission for Asia and the Pacific
EU	European Union
FAC	Fund for Aid and Co-operation
FAO	Food and Agriculture Organisation
FCO	Foreign and Commonwealth Office
FDI	Foreign direct investment
FDIC	Federal Deposit Insurance Corporation
FINNIDA	Finnish International Development Agency
FMO	Nederlandse Financierings-Maatschappij Voor Ontwikkelingslanden (Netherlands Finance Company for Developing Countries)
FSO	Fund for Special Operations
GATE	German Appropriate Technology Exchange
GATT	General Agreement on Tariffs and Trade
GDP	Gross domestic product
GNP	Gross national product
IADB	Inter-American Development Bank
IBRD	International Bank for Reconstruction and Development
IDA	International Development Association
IDB	Islamic Development Bank
IEA	International Energy Agency
IFAD	International Fund for Agriculture Development
IFC	International Finance Corporation
IFED	International Fund for External Development
IFS	International Financial Statistics
IIF	Institute for International Finance
ILO	International Labour Organisation
IMF	International Monetary Fund
IsDB	Islamic Development Bank
JERTO	Japan External Trade Organisation
JICA	Japan International Co-operation Agency
JOCV	Japan Overseas Co-operation Volunteers
KFAED	Kuwait Fund for Arab Economic Development
KfW	Kreditanstalt fur Wiederaufbau
LBFA	Libyan Bank for Foreign Assistance

LIBOR	London inter-bank offered rate
LIBID	London inter-bank bid rate
LLDCs	Least developed countries
MAMC	Managa Agricultural Management Centre
MDB	Multilateral Development Bank
MFA	Multifibre Arrangement
MIGA	Multilateral Investment Guarantee Agency
MNC	Multinational Corporation
MSACs	Most seriously affected countries
MYRA	Multiyear Rescheduling Agreement
NATO	North Atlantic Treaty Organisation
NBER	National Bureau of Economic Research
NGO	Non-governmental organisation
NIE	Newly industralised economies
NIEO	New International Economic Order
NORAD	Norwegian Agency for International Development
NTF	Nigerian Trust Fund
OAPEC	Organisation of Arab Petroleum Exporting Countries
OAU	Organisation for African Unity
OCT	Overseas countries and territories
ODA	Official development assistance
ODM	Overseas Development Ministry
OECD	Organisation for Economic Co-operation and Development
OECF	Overseas Economic Co-operation Fund
OEEC	Organisation for European Economic Co-operation
OLADE	Latin American Energy Organisation
OOF	Other official flows
OPEC	Organisation of Petroleum Exporting Countries
OPECFID	OPEC Fund for International Development
OPIC	Overseas Private Investment Corporation
PDI	Private direct investment
SAAFA	Special Arab Fund for Africa
SAF	Structural adjustment facility
SAL	Structural adjustment loan
SAMA	Saudi Arabian Monetary Agency
SAREC	Swedish Agency for Research Co-operation
SDC	Swiss Development Corporation
SDR	Special drawing rights
SELA	Sistema Economico Latinoamericano
SF	Special funds
SFD	Saudi Fund for Development
SIDA	Swedish International Development Authority

SPA	Special Programme of Assistance
TOM	Territories d'Outre-Mer
UFINEX	Union pour le Financement et l'Expansion du Commerce International
UNCDF	United Nations Capital Development Fund
UNCTAD	United Nations Conference on Trade and Development
UNDP	United Nations Development Programme
UNESCO	United Nations Educational, Scientific and Cultural Organisation
UNICEF	United Nations International Children's Emergency Fund
UNIDO	United Nations Industrial Development Organisation
UNRWA	United Nations Relief and Works Agency
USAID	United States Agency for International Development
VF	Venezuelan Fund
WEP	World Employment Programme
WFP	World Food Programme
WHO	World Health Organisation

Bibliography

Abelson, P. (1987), "Fairness in the Real World: Rules, Choices, Expectations and Policies", *Australian Economic Papers*, Vol. 26, No. 48, June 1987, pp. 1-19

Adams, Patricia (1991), *Odious Debts*, London, Earthscan

Akerlof, G. (1970), "The Market for Lemons: Qualitative Uncertainty and the Market Mechanism", *Quarterly Journal of Economics*, Vol. 84, 1970, pp. 488-500

Arrow, K. (1973), "Some Ordinalist-Utilitarian Notes on Rawls's Theory of Justice", *Journal of Philosophy*, Vol. 70, No. 9, 10 May, pp. 245-263

— (1978), "A Cautious Case for Socialism," *Dissent*, Vol. 25, pp. 472-80

Arruda, M. (1988), "The Foreign Debt and Labor in Brazil", Pries-Cono Sur, *Serie Materiales de Discusion*, No. 4

Bailey, N.A. (1983), "A Safety Net for Foreign Lending", *Business Week*, 10 January

Bailey, N.A., R.D. Luft, and R.H. Robinson (1983), "Exchange Participation Notes: An Approach to the International Financial Crisis", in *The International Financial Crisis: An Opportunity for Constructive Action*, ed. T. de Saint Phalle, Georgetown University Center for Strategic and International Studies, Washington, pp. 27-36

Baker III, J.A. (1985), Statement of the Honorable James A. Baker III, Secretary of the Treasury of the United States, before the Joint Annual Meeting of the IMF and World Bank, 8 October in *Treasury News*

Bergsten, C.F., W.R. Cline and J. Williamson (1985), *Bank Lending to Developing Countries: The Policy Alternatives*, Washington, Institute for International Economics

Blaug, M. (1978), *Economic Theory in Retrospect*, 3rd ed., Cambridge, Cambridge University Press

BIS (1979), *Manual on Statistics Compiled by International Organizations on Countries' External Indebtedness*, BIS, Basle, March

Boadway, R. and N. Bruce, (1984), *Welfare Economics*, Oxford, Basil Blackwell

Bolin, W.H. and Jorge del Canto (1983), "LDC Debt: Beyond Crisis Management", *Foreign Affairs*, Summer, pp. 1099-1112

Bradley, W. (1986), "A Proposal for Third World Debt Management", presented in Zurich, 29 June

— (1986a), "Defusing the Latin Debt Bomb", *Washington Post*, 5 October 1986

Brandt, W. et al. (1980), *North-South: A Programme for Survival*, London and Sydney, Pan Books

Brittan, S. (1988), *A Restatement of Economic Liberalism*, London, Macmillan

Cartagena Group, (1984), "The Cartagena Proposal", Address by President Belisario Betancur of Colombia, at the inauguration of Ministers of Foreign Affairs and Treasury, Cartagena, Colombia, 21 June

—, (1985)

Clark, J. (1987), "An NGO Reaction to the World Bank Paper 'Protecting the Poor during Periods of Adjustment' ", Mimeo, Oxford, Oxfam, 20 February

Cline, W.R. (1983), *International Debt and the Stability of the World Economy*, Washington, Institute for International Economics

— (1984), *International Debt: Systematic Risk and Policy Response*, Washington DC, Institute for International Economics

— (1988), "International Debt: Progress and Strategy", *Finance and Development*, June

Cohen, D. (1985), "How to Assess the Solvency of an Indebted Nation", *Economic Policy*, November

Cornia, G. (1987a), "Economic Decline and Human Welfare in the First Half of the 1980s", in UNICEF (1987), pp. 11-47

— (1987b), "Adjustment Policies 1980-85: Effects on Child Welfare", in UNICEF (1987), pp. 48-72

Culpeper, R. (1987), "Beyond Baker: The Maturing Debt Crisis", *North-South Institute Briefing*, May, pp. 18-24

CTS/CAFOD (1987), *Africa's Crisis and the Church in Britain*, London

Das, D.K. (1986), *Migration of Financial Resources to Developing Countries*, London, Macmillan

de Carmoy, H. (1987), "A Proposal for Dealing with the Debt Problem", Paper prepared for 1987 Trilateral Commission Task Force on Restoring Growth in the Debt-Laden Third World, New York, Trilateral Commission

Dias Carneiro, D. (1988), "Brazil and the IMF: Logic and Story of a Stalemate", in *Managing World Debt*, ed. S. Griffith-Jones, Harvester, Wheatsheaf

Dornbusch, R. (1987), "Our LDC Debts", *NBER Working Paper* No. 2138, January

— (1988), "Solutions to the Developing Country Debt Problem, Mimeo, Cambridge, MIT

Dornbusch, R. & S. Fischer (1984), *The World Debt Problem*, Report prepared for UNDP/UNCTAD and the Group of 24, Cambridge, MIT

The Economist (1983), "Facility to Finance the Balance of Payments Deficit caused by the Rise in Interest Rates", 2 April

— (1988), "Forgiving the Debtors", 29 October, pp 10-11

— (1989), "Of Debt and Democracy", 11 February, pp. 13, 14

— (1990), "Development Brief: The Human Condition", 26 May, p. 78

Edwards, S. (1988), "Structural Adjustment Policies in Highly Indebted Countries", *NBER Working Paper* No. 2502, February

Feldstein, M. et al. (1987), "Restoring Growth in the Debt-Laden Third World", *Triangle Paper* 33, Trilateral Commission

Fidler, S. (1988), "Third Phase of Crisis Approaches", *The Financial Times*, 28 September

Goureaux, L.M. (1980), "Compensatory Financing Facility", IMF Pamphlet Series, No. 34, Washington DC

Graff, J. de von (1957), *Theoretical Welfare Economics*, Cambridge, Cambridge University Press

Green, R.H. and S. Griffith-Jones (1986), "External Debt: Sub-Saharan Africa's Emerging Iceberg", in *Crisis and Recovery in Sub-Saharan Africa*, ed. T. Rose, Paris, OECD

Griffin, K. (1988), "Would Default on the International Debt be in the Common Interest of the North and South?", in Lima Conference (1988), pp. 87-91

Griffith-Jones, S. (1986), "Ways Forward from the Debt Crisis", *Oxford Review of Economic Policy*, Vol. 2, No. 1, Spring

— (1988), *Managing World Debt*, Harvester Wheatsheaf

Grubel, H.G. (1979), "A proposal for the Establishment of an International Deposit Insurance Corporation", *Essays in International Finance*, No. 133, Princeton, Princeton University

Guitan, M. (1982), "Economic Management and IMF Conditionality", in Killick (ed.), 1982

Guttentag, J. & R. Herring (1985), *The Current Crisis in International Banking*, Washington, Brookings Institute

Haq, M. ul (1984), "Proposal for an IMF Debt Refinancing Facility", Address to UNESCO, 6 July 1984

Harvey, C. (1981), "On Reducing the Risk in Foreign Finance - for Both Parties", London, Institute of Development Studies Discussion Paper, 1981

Helleiner, G. and F. Stewart (1987), "The International System and the Protection of the Vulnerable", in UNICEF (1987), pp. 273-298

Hope, N. (1985), "Information for External Debt Management: The Debtor Reporting System of the World Bank", in *External Debt Management*, ed. H. Mehran, pp. 174-187

International Monetary Fund (1986), "Fund-supported Programs, Fiscal Policy and Income Distribution", Occasional Paper 46, Washington DC

— (1988), *World Economic Outlook: A Survey by the Staff of the IMF*, Washington DC, April

— (1990), *World Economic Outlook: A Survey by the Staff of the IMF*, Washington DC, May

Irish Times, The (1989), "US Plans to Forgive Third World Debts", 11 March, p.6

Kenen, P.B. (1983), "Third World Debt: Sharing the Burden, A Bailout for the Banks", *New York Times*, 6 March

— (1990), "Organizing Debt Relief: The Need for a New Institution", *Journal of Economic Perspectives*, Vol. 4, No. 1, Winter, pp. 7-18

Khan, M. and M. Knight (1985), *Fund Supported Adjustment Programs and Economic Growth*, Washington DC, IMF Occasional Paper No. 41

Killick, T., ed., (1982), *Adjustment and Financing in the Developing World*, Washington DC, IMF

— (1984), *The Quest for Economic Stabilization: The IMF and the Third World*, London, Heinemann

Killick, T. and M. Martin (1989), "African Debt: The Search for Solutions", UN Africa Recovery Programme Briefing Paper, No. 1, June

Korner, P., G. Maass, T. Siebold and R. Tetzlaff (1984), *The IMF and Debt Crisis: A Guide to the Third World's Dilemma*, London, Zed Books

Krugman, P.R. (1985), "International Debt Strategies in an Uncertain World", in Cuddington and Smith, eds. *The International Debt Problem*, Washington DC, World Bank

Landell-Mills, J. (1986), *The Fund's International Banking Statistics*, Washington DC, IMF

Lessard, D.R. and J. Williamson (1985), *Financial Intermediation Beyond the Debt Crisis*, Washington DC, Institute for International Economics, September

Lever, H. and C. Huhne (1985), *Debt and Danger: The World Financial Crisis*, Harmondsworth, Penguin

Lima Conference (1988), *The External Debt, Development and International Cooperation*, Proceedings of a Conference on Non-Governmental Organizations, Lima, Peru, 25-29 January 1988, L'Harmatttan

Lomax, D.L. (1986), *The Developing Country Debt Crisis*, London, Macmillan

Massad, C. & R. Zahler (1984), "The Process of Adjustment in the Eighties: The Need for a Global Approach", *ECLA Review*, 23 August

Mehran, H. (1985), *External Debt Management*, Papers presented at a seminar organised by the IMF Institute and the Central Banking Department of the IMF, Washington, December 1984, IMF, Washington DC

Metzinger, L. (1988), "The Ethics of Economic Principles", in Lima Conference (1988), pp. 173-175

Mistry, P. (1989), "Perspectives for Campaigning on Official Debt and on African Debt in Particular", Paper presented to a Meeting of European NGOs, 30-31 August 1989

Morris D., (1979), *Measuring the Condition of the World's Poor: The Physical Quality of Life Index*, New York, Pergamon Press for the Overseas Development Council

Musgrave, R. (1959), *The Theory of Public Finance*, New York, McGraw-Hill

Nozick, R. (1974), *Anarchy, State and Utopia*, Oxford, Basil Blackwell

OECD (1987), *Economic Surveys: Ireland 1987/88*, Paris, OECD

O'Connor, J. (1985), "The Work of the IMF in External Debt Statistics", in *External Debt Management*, ed. H. Mehran, pp. 159-173

Permanent People's Tribunal (1988), "Tribunal about the Policies of the International Monetary Fund and the World Bank: Verdict, held in West Berlin, Mimeo, 26-29 September 1988

Pinstrup-Andersen, P., M. Jaramillo, and F. Stewart, (1987), "The Impact on Government Expenditure", in UNICEF (1987), pp. 73-89

Pontifical Commission Report (1987), "At the Service of the Human Community: An Ethical Approach to the International Debt Question", Pontifical Commission "Iustitia et Pax", Vatican Polyglot Press, January

Portes, R. (1986), "Sovereign Borrowing, Debt and Default: The Lessons of History for Current Policies", The O'Brien Lecture, UCD, 15 May

Rawls, J. (1973), "Distributive Justice", in E. Phelps, editor, *Economic Justice*, Penguin

Roberts, Paul Craig (1989), "No Relief on Latin Debt - Without World Bank Reform", *Business Week*, 6 March, p.11

Robichek, W. (1985), External Debt Relief, *Journal of Development Planning*, No. 16

Robinson III, J.D. (1988), "A Comprehensive Agenda for LDC Debt and World Trade Growth: Including a Proposal for an Institute of International Debt and Development", *The AMEX Bank Review*, Special Papers, No. 13, March

Rohatyn, F. (1983), Testimony before the US Congress, Senate Committee on Foreign Relations, 98 Congress, First Session, 17 January 1983

Rohatyn, F. (1983a), A Plan for Stretching out Global Debt, *Business Week*, 28 February

Rothschild, M. and J. Stiglitz (1976), Equilibrium in Competitive Insurance Markets, *Quarterly Journal of Economics*, Vol. 90, 1976, pp. 629-650

Sachs, J. D. (1988), Program Report on Developing Country Debt, *NBER Reporter*, Winter 1987/88

Schumer, C.E. (1983), "Flexibility is the Answer", *Journal of Commerce*, 13 April

Selim, H.M. (1983), *Development Assistance Policies and the Performance of Aid Agencies*, London, Macmillan

Soros, G. (1984), "The International Debt Problem: A Prescription", New York, Morgan Stanley Investment Research Memorandum

Susukuu (1987), "Can the Poor be Protected against Adjustment Programmes, Susukuu's Response to the World Bank", Mimeo, Paper Presented at UN-NGO Workshop on "Debt, Adjustment and the Needs of the Poor", Oxford, 19-22 September 1987

UNICEF (1987), *Adjustment with a Human Face: Volume 1 - Protecting the Vulnerable and Promoting Growth*, eds. G.A. Cornia, R. Jolly and F. Stewart, Oxford, Clarendon Press

UNICEF (1988), *Adjustment with a Human Face: Volume 2 - Ten Country Case Studies*, eds. G.A. Cornia, R. Jolly and F. Stewart, Oxford, Clarendon Press

United Nations Economic Commission for Latin America and the Caribbean, (1986), *Latin American and Caribbean Development: Obstacles, Requirements and Options*, New York, November

Wildstrom, Stephen, ed. (1989), "The Debt Plan Brady Floated is Still, Well, Floating", Washington Column, *Business Week*, 8 May, p. 39

Williamson, J. (1988), *Voluntary Approaches to Debt Relief*, Paper 25, Institute for International Economics, September

Witeveen, J.H. (1983), "Developing a New International Monetary System: A Long Term View", Per Jacobsson Lecture, September

World Bank (1987), "Protecting the Poor during Periods of Adjustment", Paper Prepared by World Bank Staff for Consideration by the Development Committee at April 1987 Meeting, Mimeo

Zombanakis, M. (1983), "A Way to Avoid a Crash", *The Economist*, 30 April

Index

Abelson, P. 84, 85
Adams, Patricia 83
adjustment with a human face
    74-6
adjustment with growth 29, 54,
    70, 71
African Development Bank 125,
    127
American Association of Jurists
    73
Argentina 22, 35, 40, 43, 109
Arrow, Kenneth 85, 89, 92
Asian Development Bank 125,
    128
asset egalitarianism 85, 89

Bailey, N.A. 50-1
Baker, James 38, 56-8
Baker Plan: adjustment with
    growth 29, 70, 71; outline
    56-8; resources outflow 96-
    7; trust fund 57
balance of payments 17, 21-2,
    28, 69
balance of trade 22
Bank for Intl Settlements 41,
    117
basic needs 102
bisque clauses 51
Blaug, Mark 92
Bolin, William 45
Bradley, Bill 54-5
Brady, Nicholas 38, 60-2
Brady Plan: co-financing 46, 60-
    2, 71; criticism 105; debt
    reduction 10, 19;
    IMF/World Bank
    involvement 104; statement
    76
Brazil 19, 22, 40, 43, 109
Bretton Woods 69, 125
Brittan, Samuel 83, 84
Bulow, Jeremy 97
Bush, George 10, 60

cancellations 20
capital flight 38, 109, 115
capitalisation 47
Caribbean Development Bank
    125, 128
Catholic Church 13, 66-8
Catholic Conference
    Administrative Board 68
centrally planned economies
    124-5
child mortality 10, 35
Chile 43, 46,
claims ownership 51-4
claims value 54-6
Clark, John 71
Cline, W.R. 40, 41, 42, 44,
    47
compensatory financing
    facility 50
conditionality 101-2
consumer price index 17
Coordination Committee
    104-5, 106-8, 114
Cornia, G. 32, 33, 75
Costa Rica 62
Council for Mutual Economic
    Assistance 24, 118, 125

de Carmoy, Hervé 52
defeasement 55-6, 63
de Larosiere, Jacques 42
del Canto, Jorge 45
Development Assistance
    Committee 24, 121, 122,
    123
de von Graff, T. 88
direct private investment 24
Dornbusch, Rudiger 38, 48-9,
    54, 95, 97, 107

Economic Commission for
    Asia & Far East 128

Economic Commission for
    Latin America 48
Economist, The 50
efficiency 86-8, 91, 99, 113
Enterprise for the Americas
    10, 110
equity criteria 86-90
equity swaps 49-50, 106
exchange participation notes
    51
exit bond 55, 60
expenditure switching 29-30

fairness: concept 79-92;
    current proposals 95-110;
    equity 86-90; outcome
    view 85-6; rights/process
    82-5
Federal Reserve System 42, 45
Feldstein, M. 37, 103
Fischer, S. 54
food subsidies 10
Foreign Immunities Act 100

Garcia, Alan 51
GDP ratio 16
General Agreement on Tariffs
    and Trade 12, 38
Gini concentration ratio 33
Griffin, Keith 72-3
Grubel, H.G. 45
Guinea-Bissau 20
Gulf War 59
Gutentag, Jack 44, 46

Harvey, C. 51
Hattersley, Roy 92
heavily indebted countries:
    current account 29;
    external debt 18-25;
    GDP growth 21; IMF/WB
    grouping 18; indicators 20;
    middle income countries
    57; trade balance 29
Herring, Richard 44, 46

horizontal equity 90, 92, 108,
    113
Human Development Index
    28, 35, 102

incremental official lender 52
Indebted Countries Union 72
Institute of Intl Debt &
    Development 54
Institute of Intl Finance 119
Inter-American Development
    Bank 125, 128
interest capping 47-8
interest service flow 46-9
Intl Bank for Reconstruction
    & Development 125 (see
    also World Bank)
Intl Debt Discount
    Corporation 52-3,
Intl Deposit Insurance
    Corporation 45
Intl Development Association
    119, 125, 126-7
Intl Finance Corporation 119,
    126
Intl Lending Agency 52
Intl Monetary Fund:
    compensatory financing 50;
    functions 127; programme
    extension 21; net transfers
    22; rescue packages 40-1;
    statistics 117-8; structural
    adjustment 11; total debt
    15-16; Trust Fund 57-9
Intl Monetary Fund/World
    Bank: adjustment 21; Brady
    Plan 60; coordination
    committee 114; country
    groups 18-19; Institute of
    Intl Debt & Development
    54; multilateral debt 24;
    Permanent People's
    Tribunal 73-4; policy 69-
    71, 82; publications 119;
    Seoul meeting 56-8;

Washington meetings 59,
61, 62
intl statistics 117-20
Ireland 35

jubilee year 83

Kenen, Peter 52-3, 62, 97, 99,
106
Killick, T. 33
Krugman, Paul 97

Laffer curve 97, 98-9, 105,
111
Lever, Harold 45, 52
life expectancy 35
Lomé 38, 110
London Club 40,
London intl bank offered rate
16, 42
Luft, R.D. 50-1

Madagascar 21
maximin principle 89, 91
Mexico: Brady Plan 20, 61-2;
capital flight 109; debt
swaps 61; defeasement
55-6; suspends payments
15; rescheduling 42; rescue
package 40-1; restructuring
43; World Bank 46;
Mitterand, Francois 58
Moody's 62
moral hazard 44-5
moratorium 20, 56
Morgan Guaranty 109, 119
Morocco 20
Mozambique 21, 43
multi-year rescheduling 41-4
needs indicators 28, 35-6
New York Club 40
Nicaragua 82
Niger 21
Nigeria 43, 51

non-governmental
organisations 13, 71-4
North America Free Trade
Agreement 109
Nozick, Robert 83-4

odious debts 83
official development assistance
24, 123-5
official takeover 52-4
oil crisis 9
Organisation for Economic
Cooperation and
Development 24, 59, 117,
118, 121, 123
Organisation of Petroleum
Exporting Countries 9,
110, 115, 122, 123-4
overhang hypothesis 97-9,
113
Overseas Development
Council 28, 35
Oxfam 71

Pareto principle 86, 87, 88,
98
Paris Club 20, 40, 42, 59
Permanent People's Tribunal
73-4, 82, 90
Peru 22, 51
Philippines 43,
Physical Quality of Life Index
28, 35
Pinstrup-Andersen, J. 34
Pontifical Commission for
Justice and Peace 65-8
Portugal 35
procedural reform 39-46
protectionism 38
Rawls, John 89, 91
reduction: approach 100-3;
case for 96, 100;
instruments 19-20;
implementation 103-8;
refinancing subsidiary 52
Regling, K.P. 39, 44

repayment flexibility 50-1
repudiation 55-6
rescheduling 9, 20, 39, 40-4
resources outflow 96-7
risk reduction 44-6
Robinson, J.D. 53
Robinson, R.H. 53-4
Rogoff, K. 97
Rohatyn, Felix 43-4, 52-5

Sachs, Jeffrey 97
Schumer, Charles 54
secondary markets 49-51
securitisation 44
service payments 16
service ratios 20
severely indebted LICs 58, 59
Sistema Economico
    Latinoamericano 51
social welfare function 88-9
structural adjustment: costs
    17, 27, 30-6; debt crisis 11;
    Mexico 20; policies 27, 31;
    Susukuu 71-2; World Bank
    71
Sub-Saharan Africa: current
    account 22, 29; debt
    service ratios 17-22;
    external debt 23; indicators
    20; infant mortality 35;
    problem debtors 38;
    reduction 99; special cases
    20; trade balance 29
subsistence indices 102
Sudan 22, 42
Summers, Laurence 77
Susukuu 71-2

taxation 85, 90
Toronto Summit 21, 38, 58, 59

Toronto terms 59-60, 103
Trinidad terms 59-60

ul Haq, Mahbub 52
UN Conference on Trade &
    Development 20, 119
UN Development Programme
    28, 35, 119, 128
UN Expanded Programme of
    Technical Assistance 128
UNICEF 74-6, 97, 102
UN Industrial Development
    Organisation 119
UN Special Fund 128-9
Uruguay 43
utilitarian ethic 89

Venezuela 43
vertical equity 91, 113
Volcker, Paul 42

Wallich, Henry 45, 48
Williamson, J. 55, 100
Witeveen, Johannes 45
World Bank: cofinancing 46;
    conversions 50; debtor
    reporting 118-9; heavily
    indebted countries 19;
    lending policy 125-6; net
    disbursements 36; NGOs
    71-2; programme extension
    21; special programme
    58-9; statistics 117-9;
    structural adjustment 11
World Health Organisation
    34, 104, 114

Yugoslavia 40, 41

Zambia 21
Zombanakis, Minos 45

Trócaire World Topics

A series on aspects of Third World affairs for the general reader – factual, accurate and up to date.

1. Bread and Freedom: Basic Human Needs and Human Rights
John Grindle

Basic needs – food, shelter, water, health, education, a living income and security – are the minimum human entitlement. *Bread and Freedom* outlines an approach to development which could provide these basic needs for all.

Political freedom and basic needs are inseparable. While great advances have been made in the Third World more progress is possible at little cost. All that is lacking is political will.

John Grindle has worked as an economic consultant in several developing countries and for the Irish Government.

"Some valuable ideas" *Sunday Tribune*

Trócaire and Gill and Macmillan, 1992,
£4.99, 0 7171 1967 X

2. Ireland and Latin America: Links and Lessons
Peadar Kirby

Our links with Latin America have always been strong through Irish missionaries, traders and soldiers. Part One of this book is a concise history of the region from pre-Columbus days to independence, military rule and democracy.

Part Two tells the story of leading Irish migrants to Latin America and Church and solidarity links. The author suggests Ireland and Latin America have much in common: both need to overcome a colonial legacy and find the right development model. Each can learn much from the other.

Peadar Kirby, a journalist and author, has written widely on Third World development.

"a valuable insight ... a fine read" *Sunday Tribune*
"a compact account" *Sunday Independent*
"fascinating and very readable" *Irish Catholic*

Trócaire and Gill and Macmillan, 1992,
£4.99, 0 7171 1969 6

3. The Poor Relation: Irish Foreign Policy and the Third World

Michael Holmes, Nicholas Rees, Bernadette Whelan

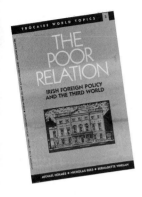

Does Ireland have an overall foreign policy towards the Third World and, if so, who decides it? How great is EC influence on that policy? Do Irish decision-makers really care about the Third World? These are some of the questions this book tackles.

The authors argue for wider consultation on policy making. They also urge Ireland to adopt a more planned approach rather than reacting to events as they happen.

Michael Holmes lectures in the Department of Politics, UCD; Nicholas Rees lectures in European Studies and International Relations at the University of Limerick. Bernadette Whelan lectures in Modern History at the University of Limerick.

Trócaire and Gill and Macmillan, 1992, £4.99, 0 7171 1970 X